why social media matters

School Communication in the Digital Age

Kitty Porterfield
Meg Carnes

Solution Tree | Press

a division of

Solution Tree

A Joint Publication With

AASA
THE SCHOOL SUPERINTENDENTS ASSOCIATION

28024

P-CO
PS835
2012

555 North Morton Street
Bloomington, IN 47404
800.733.6786 (toll free) / 812.336.7700
FAX: 812.336.7790
email: info@solution-tree.com
solution-tree.com

Printed in the United States of America
16 15 14   2 3 4 5

FSC
www.fsc.org
MIX
Paper from
responsible sources
FSC® C011935

Library of Congress Cataloging-in-Publication Data

Porterfield, Kitty, 1941-
  Why social media matters : school communication in the digital age / Kitty
Porterfield, Meg Carnes.
     p. cm.
  Includes bibliographical references and index.
  ISBN 978-1-935542-96-4 (perfect bound) -- ISBN 978-1-935542-97-1
(library edition) 1. School administrators--Professional relationships. 2.
Communication in education. 3. Public relations. I. Carnes, Meg, 1951- II.
Title.
  LB2831.8.P66 2012
  371.102'2--dc23
                          2012001888

Solution Tree
Jeffrey C. Jones, CEO
Edmund M. Ackerman, President

Solution Tree Press
President: Douglas M. Rife
Publisher: Robert D. Clouse
Vice President of Production: Gretchen Knapp
Managing Production Editor: Caroline Wise
Senior Production Editor: Suzanne Kraszewski
Proofreader: Elisabeth Abrams
Cover and Text Designer: Rian Anderson

For our moms
Kay Burnett
and
Rita Carnes
who, each in her own way,
taught us the power of
good communication.

Acknowledgments

We are, as we always are, indebted to the educators, both in schools and elsewhere in the education universe, who continue to share their wisdom with us—in particular, our friends and colleagues of the American Association of School Administrators and our school public relations colleagues from the National School Public Relations Association (NSPRA) and its regional affiliate, the Chesapeake Chapter of NSPRA (CHESPRA). It is our privilege to work with these professionals who care so deeply about public education and who serve children so faithfully.

In conducting the research for this book, we talked with many superintendents and principals and other school leaders who were most generous with their time and stories. They include David Britten, Fred Ellis, Nicole Kirby, Jill Kurtz, John Carver, Pam Moran, Charles Maranzano, Steve Hockett, Quintin Shepherd, and Sharon Trisler. These are the folks who early recognized the potential of social media communication for schools and took the risks to try. They are blazing the trail for the rest of us to follow.

We offer a big thank you to Solution Tree Press—particularly to Robb Clouse and our editor Suzanne Kraszewski. Everyone there has offered us nothing but encouragement for this project from the beginning of our relationship. We are grateful for the good care they have taken of us.

Finally, a tip of the hat to our families—Meg's husband Charlie and Kitty's (very grown up) kids, Karen, Deborah, and Michael, for their support and love. We couldn't have done it without them.

Solution Tree Press would like to thank the following reviewers:

Melissa Badger
Community and School Relations
Beloit School District
Beloit, Wisconsin

Connie Bouwman
Assistant Superintendent, Learning Services
Littleton Public Schools
Littleton, Colorado

William Clark
Superintendent
Manheim Central School District
Manheim, Pennsylvania

Deron Durflinger
Principal
Van Meter Secondary School
Van Meter, Iowa

Lance Fusarelli
Professor, Leadership Policy and Adult and Higher Education
North Carolina State University
Raleigh, North Carolina

Adam Garry
Manager, Global Professional Learning
Dell
Cary, North Carolina

James E. Grunig and Larissa A. Grunig
Professors Emeriti, Department of Communication
University of Maryland
College Park, Maryland

Chris Kennedy
Superintendent
West Vancouver School District
West Vancouver, British Columbia, Canada

Patrick Larkin
Principal
Burlington High School
Burlington, Massachusetts

Charles Maranzano, Jr.
Superintendent
Hopatcong Borough Schools
Hopatcong, New Jersey

Dave Meister
Director
Paris Cooperative High School
Paris, Illinois

Melinda Miller
Principal
Willard East Elementary
Willard, Missouri

Patricia Neudecker
Superintendent
Oconomowoc Area School District
Oconomowoc, Wisconsin

George Pawlas
Professor, Educational Leadership
University of Central Florida
Orlando, Florida

Tracey Saxon
Assistant Principal
Sutherland Middle School
Charlottesville, Virginia

Table of Contents

Visit **go.solution-tree.com/technology** for links to the resources in this book.

CHAPTER 3

Leading the Change 31

CHAPTER 4

Planning Your Debut and Creating an
Online Platform 45

CHAPTER 8

Crafting Social Media Guidelines

CHAPTER 9

What We Say and How We Say It Matter

About the Authors

 **Kitty Porterfield** is a partner in Porterfield & Carnes Communications, a consulting practice focused on building relationships between schools and community.

Kitty spent nearly thirty years directing programs and communications efforts in three school divisions in northern Virginia. She was director of communications for both the Fairfax County Public Schools and the Alexandria City Public Schools, and she directed school-community programs in both the Alexandria schools and the Arlington County Schools.

She and her communications teams received regional and national awards for print, video, and web communications, including the National School Public Relations Association Gold Medallion and the Mariner Award for Exceptional Leadership. Her crisis communication work received recognition from the U.S. Departments of Education and Homeland Security.

She and her colleague, Meg Carnes, are coauthors of *Why School Communication Matters: Strategies From PR Professionals* (2008). Kitty has written about education leadership and communication for education journals and has presented frequently at regional and national public relations and education conferences. She is a member of the National School Public Relations Association (NSPRA), the American Association of School Administrators (AASA) and the Chesapeake Chapter of NSPRA (CHESPRA). She has served as chair of CHESPRA and of the Northern Virginia Community College Board. She is currently vice president of the Literacy Council of Northern Virginia.

Kitty is a graduate of Radcliffe College, Harvard University, with a degree in government. She lives in northern Virginia.

To learn more about Kitty, visit www.porterfieldandcarnes.com.

 **Meg Carnes** is a partner in Porterfield & Carnes Communications, a consulting practice focused on building relationships between schools and community.

Meg spent over twenty-five years in K–12 public education. She taught English and was the department chair at a high school in upstate New York where she was also an adjunct instructor at Syracuse University. She also taught high school journalism, advised a national award-winning newspaper, and was an adjunct instructor at Northern Virginia Community College. She later worked as a communications specialist for Fairfax County (Virginia) Public Schools when the school division was awarded the Gold Medallion for communication excellence from the National School Public Relations Association (NSPRA).

Along with her colleague Kitty Porterfield, Meg is coauthor of *Why School Communication Matters: Strategies From PR Professionals* (2008). She has written about communication for education journals and is a frequent presenter at national public relations and education conferences. She has evaluated school division communications programs for national competitions. She is a member of the National School Public Relations Association, the American Association of School Administrators (AASA), and the Chesapeake Chapter of NSPRA (CHESPRA). She has served on the CHESPRA Board and on NSPRA committees.

Meg is a graduate of Syracuse University with an advanced degree in journalism and holds a Certificate of Advanced Studies in educational administration from the State University of New York. She has received the APR (Accreditation in Public Relations).

To learn more about Meg, visit her at porterfieldandcarnes.com. You can follow Kitty and Meg on Twitter @12CommSOS.

To book Kitty or Meg for professional development, contact pd@solution-tree.com.

Foreword

Daniel A. Domenech, Executive Director of the
American Association of School Administrators

I was a thirty-something superintendent in the late 1970s when I purchased a set of Commodore PET 8k computers for my schools in Deer Park, New York. You couldn't do much with them except program them to perform simple functions and games (Space Invaders was a favorite); word processing was not even a reality back then. Needless to say, the world has changed dramatically since I bought those computers; today, toys in cereal boxes come with more computing power than the Commodore PET, and computers have transitioned from our desktops to the palms of our hands to revolutionize how we communicate and when.

Skill in communication is a key ingredient for school leaders' success in today's complex education environment, and this communication now includes social media. Social media tools are incredibly powerful, and many educators are grappling with the reality that social media has become the standard for communication for a new generation of students and parents. Kids do not talk anymore—they text. People maintain relationships solely via Facebook. Information about our schools travels through the Internet at incredible speed, promulgated by students, parents, staff, and members of the community. Educators can either learn to use these powerful tools or stand hopelessly by as the information—good and bad—swirls around them. Ultimately, whether we choose to use the medium or not, we must be familiar with it and aware of what it can do—both *for* us and *to* us.

Regardless of your level of technological literacy, this book will help you understand and navigate the intricate world of today's social media and the challenges and opportunities it poses for our schools.

I met Kitty Porterfield and Meg Carnes when I became superintendent of schools in Fairfax County, Virginia, in 1997. Since then, they have been invaluable resources in helping me communicate with all segments of my school community and beyond. Together, Kitty, Meg, and I have managed through the changes brought on by technological advances. This book focuses on the latest communication challenge educators and our schools face—school communications in the digital age.

Kitty and Meg explore and explain the many facets of social media and the issues surrounding it to help you make the best decisions for your situation. "To tweet or not to tweet, that is the question." Indeed, school leaders wonder, Should we have a Facebook page or blog, or both? How interactive should our webpage be? The authors guide you through lessons about social media sites and tools and how to use them most effectively. I have greatly benefitted from their expertise, and with this book, you can too.

Given the speed of change in technology, this up-to-date book is a must for all school leaders who want to learn about today's social media and how to most effectively use it to communicate with their stakeholders.

Introduction

In his review of *The Twitter Book* (2009), by Tim O'Reilly and Sarah Milstein, Steve Rubel (2011), director of insights at Edelman Digital, likens a journey into social media to a journey into Nepal:

> Ever been to Nepal? Me neither. However if I ever do go . . . I will enlist a Sherpa to guide me through the landscape and the nuances of the culture.

We have written *Why Social Media Matters: School Communication in the Digital Age* to be your Sherpa on your journey into the new world of social media—a journey that can be exciting, interesting, baffling, challenging, and ultimately rewarding.

School leaders have often been slow to venture into the realm of new media, perhaps fearing that social media and other tools will turn out to be passing fads or, at best, just a way to play or find old friends. We know too many school leaders who continue to ignore tools like Facebook, YouTube, and Twitter. They tell us, "We don't understand what these things are and what they are supposed to do for us." For these leaders, investing in new media might seem like a waste of time and money; however, nothing could be further from the truth.

Times have changed. In today's world, it is no longer enough to do a good job teaching the young people in our schools. Educators must also take care to build and sustain trusting relationships with students' families and with the taxpayers in the communities they serve. School leaders have a responsibility to reach out to the larger community—to listen to their stakeholders and include them in the life of the school in new ways, to provide information more quickly than ever before, and ultimately, to build stakeholder trust. To do this, leaders must develop new communication skills that utilize new technologies.

Educators used to communicate by sending messages *out* to parents and the community; now, we live in an age in which information is shared—not just distributed—and two-way communication is expected. Just as rows of desks nailed to the floor and September-to-June school calendars are remnants of education in a nineteenth-century agrarian society, the six-panel, four-color, two-fold brochure and monthly paper newsletters are the remnants of a twentieth-century view of adequate school communication. We contend that social media tools—although admittedly imperfect—are necessary to meet the demands of school communities today.

Three Goals

In this book, we have tried to accomplish three goals:

1. We explore the communication landscape in which we all are operating. How did we get here? Why has social media become so important? Who is part of our network? Why is it critical that schools get with the program? What happens if they don't? It is our belief that to use social media well, you have to understand something about *why* it is so powerful and how you can get the most out of it.

2. We explore the process of how to plan your social media debut and how to create an online platform. We lay out step-by-step instructions on the basic mechanics of three popular tools of social media: Twitter, Facebook, and blogs. We describe how to send a Tweet, create a Facebook page for your school or district, and develop a blog. These chapters are meant to help a novice get his or her feet wet, so to speak. They also offer examples of how these platforms can work to support teaching and learning in your schools or district.

3. We look at the content leaders are communicating. Communication is only as powerful as the strength of its messages. It is easy to become enamored with the communication process and forget what it is we are trying to say. Your stakeholders ask you to deliver important information in a transparent way. Whether you are speaking face-to-face to members of the Parent-Teacher-Student Association or posting on Facebook, content is the key to getting the right message out.

This book is not meant to be an encyclopedia of social media; rather, it is intended to make you think and give you a place to begin. You can read this book cover to cover or piece by piece. Jump in to a topic that intrigues you and work your way around. When teaching a new subject to students, teachers often use hooks to draw students in. Find your hook. What sounds familiar? What knowledge do you already have that you can build on? Be patient with yourself. After all, you are learning something brand new, something that may seem completely foreign and counterintuitive.

This book contains how-to instructions, best practices, practical suggestions, and some cautionary tales about using social media to support the communication efforts in your school or district. This is not a book about using technology in the classroom with children, although we believe that to be an equally urgent and important task. Our goal is to help you create a meaningful framework for using social media to improve your communication with staff members, parents, and the larger community with an emphasis on what will work for you in your unique situation.

Hold Tight or Let Go?

School leaders spend time and energy leading their communities through all kinds of changes—changes in faculty, instruction, administration, and boundaries, to name a few. Now, new technology and social media networks have introduced a completely new set of changes that educators must reckon with. Moving forward can be painful. Change can make us feel uncomfortable. We might feel as though there is little solid ground beneath our feet. Our response is often to hold tight to what we have.

What we suggest is that, rather than draw the shades, school leaders need to step out boldly to meet new challenges. The Wright brothers didn't get off the ground by doing things the way they had always been done. Likewise, once you get your wings, we think you will enjoy the flight—and we know you will see the communication landscape (and your work) from an entirely new perspective.

We encourage superintendents and principals—indeed *all* school leaders—to step forward to lead the change. We hope that *Why Social Media Matters: School Communication in the Digital Age* will help you do just that.

1 The Change

In today's world, new technologies offer new ways to communicate with stakeholders—ways that are faster, more flexible, and friendlier. These new communication tools offer school leaders a strategic advantage in their efforts to reach the community. Without question, the future and all its newfangled technologies seem to fly past us at lightning speed. We become breathless trying to keep up.

Think back to a time before social media, before the Internet was the vast place it is today—a time before email. Consider how schools and school districts notified their community about important information: they wrote press releases and mailed them to newspapers and other media outlets. Then came the fax revolution and, almost overnight, superintendents were scrambling to buy fax machines with mass distribution capabilities. Those fax machines were hardly warmed up when email emerged, and districts set to work collecting email addresses for their media contacts.

When email first began to show up on computers in school district offices, ten or twelve messages a day in your inbox felt like an avalanche. Principals and central office staff complained that they couldn't answer their email *and* get their work done too. It was one or the other, they said. Some superintendents would not allow a computer on their desk. (They considered the computer—like the typewriter before it—suitable only for an assistant.) Many teachers refused to give out their email address because they didn't want to hear from "all those parents."

Today, email *is* our work—or at least a major piece of how we get the job done. Administrators, teachers, and parents correspond regularly, and we almost expect an inbox of a hundred emails by the end of the day. Despite this, consider how much more work we accomplish today with far less effort than we did in the time of snail-mailed or faxed press releases. New technology allows us to say more and reach more people in a shorter span of time and with less effort.

Now, with the popularity and pervasiveness of the web, many schools and districts post their news on the district's website where anyone can go to browse—gone are the days of the traditional press release. Reporters scan the superintendent's blog, the district's Facebook page, and neighborhood digital bulletin boards for news. They follow the district on Twitter.

In an amazingly short period of time, social media has become an integral part of our lives: the way we conduct business, connect with our friends, shop for household items, research complicated issues, find medical help, stay abreast of the news, and plan our vacations, to name just a few. Social media tools extend our influence in the worlds that matter most to us, allow us to pass on important knowledge, and help us learn from others in ways that were never before possible. These goals are particularly critical in school leadership.

Despite this change in how we live and do business, school leaders are reluctant to embrace social media. A member survey conducted by the American Association of School Administrators (AASA) in late 2009 revealed that fewer than 20 percent of the school leaders surveyed made regular use of social media channels, including Facebook and Twitter. About 30 percent of the survey respondents had a blog, yet only about 10 percent posted on it regularly (American Association of School Administrators, 2009). Additionally, superintendents in a 2011 AASA focus group said they wanted nothing to do with social media. They perceived Facebook as potentially dangerous and intrusive (American Association of School Administrators, 2011). In addition, one superintendent humorously explained to his peers that he really didn't want to be somebody's friend.

We understand the reluctance to hop on social media channels. The concept of *friending*—the Facebook term for those who connect to your online page—is a 180-degree turn from traditional school-community communications. Moving from the comfortable framework of the monthly newsletter to a two-way online conversation seems risky and littered with what-ifs. What if I post a blog and someone writes a negative comment? What if our Facebook page results in people whining about things that we can't do anything about, like personnel issues? What if students start following our Twitter feed? None of these things can happen with traditional, safe one-way communication.

From the outside, it might be difficult to imagine how online conversations can produce anything but headaches; those who haven't yet used social media might expect the exchanges there to be draining, dispiriting, and ultimately fruitless. It feels like chaos: anyone can initiate a conversation, and the communication is not simply in writing—people can talk back and forth with each other through video, music, and voice.

Leaders might wonder if this just isn't another fad, one more bill of goods with empty promises. Many school leaders don't regard time spent on social media as valuable. How can writing a blog about themselves be as critical as their mission of student success? They just hope the whole "social media thing" will go away.

It is more than foolish for school leaders to pretend that education is somehow untouched by this new media; it is negligent, and it reinforces the image that many Americans have of schools and school leaders—that leaders keep their eyes on the rear-view mirror as they run our schools, and that our schools are just not in step with the times.

A Connected World

Consider the following points from the Pew Internet and American Life Project (Pew Research Center, 2010) about the pervasiveness of Internet use:

- Seventy-nine percent of adults use the Internet.
- Sixty-six percent of adults have broadband at home.
- Ninety percent of parents have a cell phone, compared with seventy-two percent of adults without children under eighteen at home.

The Pew Internet and American Life Project (Zickuhr, 2010) also offers the following facts about the rapid spread of social media use:

- Nearly three quarters of teens and young adults age eighteen to twenty-nine who are online use social network sites. (Note that some of them are parents of our students.)
- Social networking use among Internet users ages fifty and older had doubled—from 22 percent in 2009 to 47 percent as of December 2010.

Nine out of every ten Internet users in the United States are now visiting a social network every month, and the average Internet user is spending more than four hours on these sites each month. In fact, one of every eight minutes online is spent on Facebook (comScore, 2011). When the Queen of England has a Facebook page—and she does—you know the world has changed.

Getting and Using News

The Internet has changed the way we get our information, particularly our news. In a 2010 Pew Research Center poll, only 42 percent of Americans said they considered the television set to be a necessity, down from 64 percent in 2006, and only 62 percent considered a landline telephone to be a necessity, down from 66 percent the previous year (Taylor & Wang, 2010). Additionally, only 50 percent of Americans said they read a local newspaper, and 17 percent said they read a national newspaper like the *New York Times* or *USA Today* (Purcell, Rainie, Mitchell, Rosenstiel, & Olmstead, 2010).

However, surveys report that 93 percent of Americans use cell phones, and a third of those use their phones to browse the web and check email (Smith, 2010a). Consumers sent 1.8 trillion mobile text messages between June 2009 and June 2010 (Jayson, 2010), and in 2010, Facebook exceeded 500 million users (Pegoraro, 2011b) and pushed past Google to become the most popular site on the Internet (Mui & Whoriskey, 2010).

Interestingly enough, the research shows that the average amount of time Americans spend with the news on a given day is just as high as it was in the mid-1990s (Pew Research Center, 2010). The change is *where* Americans find their news (Purcell et al., 2010). Only 26 percent of all Americans say they read a print newspaper yesterday. If you ask adults under thirty, the percentage drops to 8 (Pew Research Center, 2010).

Today, American adults have turned into news grazers; 92 percent of them use multiple platforms to get their news, including national and local television, the Internet, national and local newspapers, and the radio. Only 7 percent of us get our news from a single media platform. We check up on what's happening whenever we have a chance (Purcell et al., 2010).

According to the Pew Research Center's Internet and American Life Project (Purcell et al., 2010) people's relationship to news is becoming increasingly more portable, personalized, and participatory. Consider the following:

- Thirty-three percent of cell phone owners now access news on their cell phones. (Netbook and tablet users swell this number.)
- Twenty-eight percent of Internet users have customized their home page to include news from sources and on topics that particularly interest them.

- Thirty-seven percent of Internet users have contributed to the creation of news, commented about it, or disseminated it via postings on social media sites like Facebook or Twitter. (Purcell et al., 2010)

According to Pew (Purcell et al., 2010), "The Internet is at the center of the story of how people's relationship to news is changing." Fifty-nine percent of Americans get their news from a combination of online and offline sources. The Internet is the third most popular news platform, behind local television news and national television news. As Purcell et al. (2010) note:

> To a great extent, people's experience of news, especially on the Internet is becoming a shared social experience as people swap links in emails, post news stories on their social networking site feeds, highlight news stories in their Tweets, and haggle over the meaning of events in discussion threads.

An example of news sharing via new technologies was evident in August 2011 when the East Coast experienced a rare earthquake. In Washington, DC, people poured out of office buildings—cell phones in hand—each reading, texting, tweeting, and emailing their own news to their friends. Later, the headlines read "Twitter Beats Gov't, Traditional Media and Geological Organizations to Break #Earthquake News" (Dugan, 2011).

There has been a change not only in how people get the news, but also in how they use it. Today, 72 percent of people say they follow the news because they "enjoy talking with friends, family about what's happening in the world." Sixty-nine percent say they follow the news because they "feel [a] special social or civic obligation to stay informed" and 61 percent "find information in news that helps improve [their] life" (Purcell et al., 2010). Social indeed. What once was subject matter for discussion and reflection around the family dinner table is now information and opinion available for immediate action. We can read reviews of the newest smartphone on our old smartphone, make a quick decision, and order the new one online. We can read about the superintendent's new redistricting plan, email the plan to our neighbors and friends, and organize a protest demonstration for tomorrow night's school board meeting.

Who Uses New Tools?

We might assume that only those who are affluent have and use new technologies, but consider the following statistics:

- Seventy-five percent of adults in households with incomes less than $30,000 have cell phones. Ninety percent of adults in households with incomes of $30,000–49,000 own a cell (Smith, 2010a). In some of these homes, a cell phone or a smartphone is the household's only Internet access.

- Nearly 60 percent of adults in households with incomes less than $30,000 have a computer, as do 84 percent of adults in households with incomes of $30,000–49,000 (Smith, 2010b).

Another misconception about new technology is that minority communities are not connected. Although the number of connected African American and Hispanic adults is not as high as it is for Caucasian adults, the gaps are not as large as once thought:

- Eighty-four percent of Hispanic adults and 79 percent of African American adults own cell phones (in comparison to 85 percent of Caucasian adults) (Smith, 2010a).

- Laptop ownership among African Americans rose dramatically in just one year—from 34 percent in 2009 to 51 percent in 2010 (Smith, 2010c).

- When minorities don't have computers at home, they often gain access at the office or fill the computer banks at local libraries.

Aaron Smith (2010c) notes that "the Internet and broadband populations have become more diverse" since the early 2000s. Both African Americans and English-speaking Latinos are more likely to use a much wider range of their cell phone's capabilities than are Caucasian users. They are more apt to use their mobile devices to text, use the

Internet, record or watch videos, use email or instant messaging, listen to music, or make a charitable donation (Smith, 2010c).

Smith's research demonstrates that minority adults outpace Caucasians in their use of social technologies. Among Internet users, seven in ten African Americans and English-speaking Latinos use social networking sites—which is significantly higher than the six in ten Caucasians who do so. And, perhaps most important for education leaders, minority Americans are also likely to use digital technologies, such as blogs, social networking sites, and neighborhood bulletin boards, to keep up with what's happening in their neighborhoods (Smith, 2010c).

We are changing the way we interact with each other and get news about the world around us. This is clear as our favorite newspapers grow thinner and increasingly focus on sensational news in search of newsstand appeal—or cease to exist altogether. Teenagers would rather text than call, and twenty-somethings no longer listen to the telephone messages we carefully leave them. Our school news is delivered to the community almost instantaneously on the neighborhood blog, far faster than we can put out a press release.

The trends are clear: more and more people are investing in new technologies, and the tools themselves are getting smaller and smaller. Computing is going mobile: mobile devices (including tablets) now make up the largest share of personal computers, with forty-eight million units projected to be sold in 2011 (Pegoraro, 2011a). Aaron Smith, a senior research specialist at the Pew Internet and American Life Project, found that access to the digital world is increasingly being untethered from the desktop (Smith, 2010c).

In a large measure, plummeting technology prices have made possible the meteoric rise in the number of communication devices in American households. In 1984, the average price of a cell phone was about $4,000. In 2000, the average was $200, and today it is less than that (Pegoraro, 2011a). In the early 80s, a deluxe Hewlett-Packard 8086 personal computer with two floppy disk drives (and software you had to load yourself) could be had for a cool $5,000.

Today, a stripped-down netbook computer can be yours for barely $250. These changes are having a profound effect on how we live.

Although all the changes and choices can be overwhelming at times, there is much to like about the new technologies and the benefits they offer. For school leaders, this transition to new technologies and social media offers tremendous opportunities to build connections with stakeholders.

Next Steps

1. Examine your school's or district's means of communication among adults. How many ways can you get information to your students, teachers, parents, and community friends? How many ways can they get messages to you?

2. List some of the key questions you have about social media. What do you hope to learn by reading this book? Who or what else can you turn to for help?

Who Are Our Stakeholders?

In 1991, social historians Bill Strauss and Neil Howe published *Generations*, a history of America since 1584, generation by generation. Together, they reviewed the research that they had each conducted over their independent careers and mapped out how entire generations of people were shaped by the great events of their time, such as the Great Depression, World War II, and the Apollo launch. These events, they claim, created groups of people of similar age who respond to life in similar ways.

Howe, Strauss, and Nadler (2008) identify four different groups of people with different characteristics, strengths, and needs working together in our school communities today: the Silent Generation, the Baby Boom Generation (Baby Boomers), Generation X (Gen Xers), and Generation Y (the Millennials). Each of these groups brings with them the hopes, the fears, and the collective experiences of their generation, making a veritable "school stew." The following feature box describes each of these groups of stakeholders.

The Generations

1. **The Silent Generation.** These folks, born between 1925 and 1942 (approximately), were raised to be seen and not heard. As they were growing up, they were influenced by World War II, the Korean War, the civil rights movement, and the antiwar movement. They came to political power during the Watergate scandal. They built enduring political institutions, but interestingly, not one of them was ever elected president. As a group, they are great proponents of discussion and collaboration. They place a high value on process.

2. **The Baby Boom Generation (also known as the Baby Boomers).** Boomers were born between 1942 and 1960. They were Dr. Spock's feed-on-demand babies, raised on postwar optimism. They scorned the old ways of their parents. They fueled Vietnam protests and partied at Woodstock. Even as adults, they remain rebellious, inner driven, and idealistic. They are risk takers. They are also helicopter parents. They are sure they know what is best for their children, and they know how to secure it.

3. **Generation X (also known as the Gen Xers).** Gen Xers were born between 1961 and 1981. They grew up in an era of failing schools, failing marriages, working mothers, and devil-child movies. They are the latchkey children. They learned early on to take care of themselves and blossomed into a generation of problem solvers. (As children, they learned which neighbors to call on when they were locked out of the house.) They thrive on collaboration. They are skeptics, realists, pragmatists—and at the same time, highly family oriented. They imagine doing things that others wouldn't dare.

4. **Generation Y (also known as the Millennials).** These men and women were born between 1981 and 2002. Some are not even out of school yet, but the oldest members of this generation are in the workforce and bringing their own children to school. These young people grew up in an era of "the wanted child." They have experienced a life focused around them. This generation is sheltered, special, confident, team oriented, conventional, pressured, and achieving. They are optimists, but they ask for constant praise and reinforcement. They look to their peers, rather than experts, for opinions and support. They have grown up with technology as an extension of themselves.

Source: Howe et al. (2008).

With this kind of diversity among your stakeholders, there are days when you need an interpreter (or a whole team of interpreters!) just to keep communication moving forward. While Gen Xers demand individualized services for their children and Millennials ask for a copy of the complete school crisis security plan, the older school staff—the Baby Boomers and members of the Silent Generation—shake their head in amazement and sometimes disgust. For them, all the old rules have gone out the window.

Understanding how each generation thinks, what its goals are, and what it values can make communicating with, leading, and motivating these groups easier. Strauss and Howe (1991; Howe et al., 2008) offer school leaders a great framework for viewing the people they encounter in their school and community and some guidelines for working successfully with all of them, generation by generation.

Strauss and Howe do not make value judgments about each group; they do not claim one generation is better than another. Rather, they explore how each group is shaped differently and responds differently. Unfortunately, in our schools and offices, we are more likely to hear judgments about these groups, such as: "These young people! They want everything *their* way!" or "Why won't you even *think* about changing? All you say is 'We've always done it that way!'" The Strauss and Howe generational framework gives us a place to start a constructive conversation about how we can do it together.

New Tools for the New Generations

So what, you ask, does all this have to do with social media? A lot. School leaders must be able to communicate with all their stakeholders, from the staff members in their buildings to the parents and other stakeholders in their communities. Remember, the younger generations are armed to the teeth with new technology: smartphones, iPhones, iPads, netbooks, and so on. The presence of Gen Xers and Millennials in our midst is changing the nature of how we do business in schools. In this new world, communicating with stakeholders both in and out of the schools becomes not just another thing to do, but rather *the* thing to do.

Gen Xer and Millennial stakeholders above all else want to be connected. They want to know what's going on *while* it's going on, not after the decisions have been made. They are looking for both hard data and context. They want to hear both rational explanations and the stories that are driving the decisions. A survey by the National School Public Relations Association (NSPRA; 2011) shows that the information parents most want from school districts is "a rationale or reasons for decisions made by the district."

Members of these groups want to draw their own conclusions and seek their own solutions. Brochures and newsletters no longer work. New technologies allow us to meet their needs. In today's world:

- **Timing is everything.** Gen Xers and Millennials like to receive news in *real time*. They work on their own schedule, not on yours. If you have posted information on your website or on Facebook (about kindergarten registration or graduation requirements, for example), these parents and other stakeholders will find the information when they have the time—and they'll be grateful to have it available when they want it.

- **Unlike their elders, these folks expect to be updated all day long with the latest news.** This group is accustomed to getting the latest information instantaneously. They do not want to wait to read new information several days after it happens; they want to know now. They want a Tweet telling them about a new school boundary proposal that sends them to the school website for more information. They want a text message when they must pick up their child from school early because of snow.

- **Young parents want choices for their children.** These stakeholders want programs that can be customized to fit their children's needs and lifestyles. New software programs that allow parents to view their student's progress online and correspond directly by email with teachers give parents a sense of participation in their child's development and a sense of confidence in the school's capabilities. They see tangible documentation that the school is closely monitoring their child, and they feel included in the education process because they can access this information immediately and have a direct connection to their child's teacher(s). They have grown up expecting access to data and the decision-making process in all aspects of their lives. They expect no less from their child's school.

- **Today's parents are far less trusting of institutions in general, and educators in particular, than the parents of previous generations.** You need to gain the trust of this group of stakeholders. This is best done by being persistent over time. Parents want data, standards, and transparency. They need you to show them how things will work for their child. They also want to build relationships with the adults who will be important in their child's life. Facebook postings that highlight and point the way to detailed test scores available on the web are one way social media tools can build trust—by providing data. A short video by a child's teacher (on Facebook, on the web, on

YouTube) introducing her- or himself and the classroom to the child and parent can provide comfort and build trust.

- **Parents, particularly Millennials, want to collaborate.** Members of this group don't see schools as the enemy; rather, they are looking to create community with the school personnel who matter in their world, and they look to their peers often for support and confirmation. School leaders can use Twitter conversations, for example, to create such community.

The New Challenge

People are living and working longer. The top end of the education workforce has delayed retirement and remains a significant presence on school employee rosters and within the community as stakeholders. The 40- and 50-year-olds, often looking for leadership roles, remain a presence. The 20- and 30-year-olds are our newest stakeholders—the parents of our newest clients and teachers early in their careers.

School leaders no longer hold all the information or decide who knows what and when. The characteristics and experiences of Gen Xers and the Millennials have created an increase in communication and information exchange that has already led to a seismic shift in responsibility and control. As a school leader, you lose some of your advantage and some of your political power. (This is not your imagination.) This new reality gives some education leaders pause.

Educator and researcher Alan November (2010) confronts that shift head on:

> It is only natural that a shift of control creates fear and anxiety. . . . The real fear lies in people's hesitancy about the changing roles necessitated by the meaningful use of the technology. It is essential that the fears and anxiety felt by those who are affected by the change not be ignored, but instead be confronted, so that the potential inherent change can also be fully explored. (p. 62)

As we've said before: the reality is, there is no going back. The shift is already happening around us. The only decision we have left is how far behind we're going to get—or how adventurous we will be.

Next Steps

1. Identify three generational clashes in your building or district. Describe the opposing values or cultures. Where is the common ground?

2. Is there one generation in your community that feels particularly underappreciated? Why? Are there any simple shifts in communication media that you could initiate that might alleviate some of this intergenerational tension?

Ten Realities of Social Media

Social media is here to stay. We no longer need to ask, "Is this just a passing fad?" It will remain in our lives in one form or another because it is the way in which the new generation communicates. Social media is a tremendous tool for reaching your parents and community members. Consider the following ten realities of social media:

1. **Social media is a new way to build relationships.** It should not be a surprise that the key to good leadership is strong relationships (see especially the work of Michael Fullan and John Kotter). Creating relationships is an ongoing job. Social media is an efficient and effective tool to help build ties to our stakeholders.

2. **Communication is no longer about you; it's about your customers.** Your parents and staff members are growing younger by the day. They are much different than their parents: they want to work in teams, be part of the solution, and hear you tell them they've done a good job. Today's parents refuse to be shut out of the education process.

3. **If you don't tell your story, someone else will.** Social media is our present-day equivalent of the front-porch, backyard-fence, and playground-bench conversation. Your stakeholders are already talking about you—on community bulletin boards, on local newspaper comment boards, on Facebook, and Twitter. Listen in, and use these opportunities to be sure that your voice is heard.

4. **Your reputation is at stake.** In the end, you are the one charged with maintaining your school's or district's good name. If you only listen to the concerns of your department heads and Parent-Teacher-Student Association leaders, you will never know the concerns of parents and other stakeholders. Social media can provide the same amount of feedback as a dozen focus groups, without all the time and effort.

5. **The response will most likely be positive.** School systems that have taken a proactive step to establish social connections, such as establishing a blog, a Twitter feed, and posting on YouTube, get high marks from their communities. Real-time conversations with the community allow leadership to become transparent. The districts that feel the brunt of viral venom are those that *don't* already have digital avenues of conversation open. If you already have friends on Facebook or Twitter, they will come to your defense when someone posts negative comments. You won't have to. Recently, in our town, for example, a noted education columnist was immediately slammed online when he (perhaps unfairly) attacked a local school system's parent visitation rule.

6. **You don't have to do it all at once.** School leaders can start small with social media with little investment of money—just time. For example, setting up a Twitter account allows you to send your short headlines (140 or fewer characters) to your stakeholders' mobile devices and computers in real time, along with links to your website for more details.

7. **Social media gives you the chance to stay ahead of the curve.** Like putting your ear to the train tracks to hear the rumble of the approaching train, social media gives you the opportunity

to respond quickly to rumors and dissention, without the filters of traditional media where only what suits editorial or economic agendas is printed. After you've established a network of social media, updating it takes less time than writing and publishing a press release—and the effects can reach much farther.

8. **It's here to stay.** The forms that social media take will keep changing as new technologies emerge, but social media itself is here to stay. Part of a school leader's job is staying abreast of the changes. People use social media because they can—it's here, it's new, it's cool—but social media also helps to fill a deep need in our communities: the need to feel connected, to be in touch.

9. **Social media helps you build community and a sense of ownership among your stakeholders.** People only invest in what they care about. In today's world, you cannot assume that anyone cares about or respects public institutions simply because they are institutions. People care when they feel cared for. A social media presence speaks to inclusion. It is an invitation to be part of the action.

10. **It takes the whole village.** We know that kids learn best when their parents and the community are invested in what goes on in our classrooms. Social media is a key part of what it takes today to win that investment.

While principals and superintendents are rearranging their organizational charts and agonizing over budget proposals, important conversations about their schools are being held all around them. These conversations used to take place at the grocery store, around the swimming pool in the summer, and at community events; now they take place on the web—on neighborhood digital bulletin boards, on Twitter, in blogs, and on YouTube. School leaders who do not participate in social media are missing out on the opportunity to hear what their stakeholders are saying.

As the statistics show, old-fashioned media is commanding less attention. Local news in general—and school news in particular—gets less and less ink and airtime. If your stakeholders are getting their news online, you will not necessarily reach them by calling a print reporter or even publishing your own print newsletter. Twenty-first century news-grazing habits call for a sea change in how school leaders approach their communication with all their stakeholders. When it comes to distributing your news, the words to remember are *portable, personalized,* and *participatory.*

For schools, the consequences of not being part of the conversation can be dire. They are the same kinds of consequences that school leaders might have suffered years ago if they were never available to meet with parents or parent groups, failed to respond to parents' requests, or did not maintain relationships with civic leaders: the superintendent or principal was labeled nonresponsive, the school lost community support or became the object of intensive media scrutiny, and the principal could be moved—or a superintendent's contract not renewed—because he or she was perceived to be "not present." The difference today is that the groundswell of discontent grows a whole lot faster online and can spread a whole lot farther.

Next Steps

1. Create a simple survey for your school or district community. Ask parents and staff members where they get news about school and whose opinions they trust. Do they like robocalls and text messages from the school? Do they read your website? Ask where they get other news. Do they read a newspaper, go online, or follow Twitter sites? Do they trust Facebook?

2. Revisit the three generational clashes you identified earlier. Do the results from your survey give you any clues about new ways to reach your stakeholders?

Key Points

Today's technologies offer faster, more flexible, and friendlier ways for school leaders to communicate messages about their schools to their stakeholders. Even though the rate at which these technologies are changing—from fax to Facebook—can be overwhelming, we cannot afford to fall behind.

Surveys document the decline of television and newspapers as the major sources of news for most Americans in our communities and the rise of the web and social media as key sources of information. Cell phones, PDAs, netbooks, laptops, and tablets—in fact, portable devices of all kinds—are taking over the communication airwaves. Although some disparities among population subgroups still exist, the gaps are closing fast. The trend for tomorrow is portable, personalized, and participatory. Schools have to keep pace.

Four distinct generations meet in today's schools and communities. Each generation has its own culture and values. Each generation thinks its way of doing business is the best way. And each has its own way of communicating. A school leader's job is to navigate the sometimes murky waters that divide the generations and to find ways of building bridges to each of them, because they all have strengths to bring to the table. The hidden challenge for the leader is that, in the process of collaboration, there will most likely be a shift in responsibility and control, but that's actually not all bad.

2 A Hyperconnected Community

Your stakeholders are engaging in social media, using it to interact and enrich their lives. They use social media to ask questions, comment on events, discuss what-ifs, and imagine possibilities. Many are optimistic and seize opportunities that improve their lives, their children's lives, and the world around them. Others use social media for negative purposes—naming names or making hurtful or unfair comments, often hiding behind anonymity. Other users lurk—actively following what is written, but not commenting. School leaders are wise to understand the many places their stakeholders go online when it comes to social media, how these forums work, and how they can be used—both for pro- and anti-school purposes.

Where Are Our Stakeholders?

Members of your community are likely to gather in the following popular online communities.

Facebook

Facebook (www.facebook.com) is a social networking service that lets you connect with others who share similar interests. Created in early 2004 by Mark Zuckerberg, then an undergraduate at Harvard

University, Facebook has grown to more than 800 million active users. It allows users to create a page or profile with a built-in sharing system. Once you post an item to your page, the people you have connected with on Facebook can leave comments on your page and discuss the item with others. Many rely on Facebook as a way to keep in touch with a wide variety of people and institutions. For that reason, it's an attractive tool for school leaders to keep in touch with their parents and community members. Many in your community will rely on Facebook more than on your website to get school news. It can also become a tool to facilitate meaningful conversations. (See chapter 5, Facebook 101, for more information about Facebook.)

Twitter

Twitter (http://twitter.com) is a tool that allows people to communicate and stay connected through the exchange of brief (no more than 140 characters) messages that answer one simple question: What are you doing? Tweets have evolved from documenting everyday experiences ("I had a ham sandwich for lunch") to now offering interesting and valuable content around important topics with links to related content on the web. Twitter is a tool people often utilize to broadcast their experiences to the world when they are in the midst of a newsworthy event, such as a crisis or natural disaster. As a Twitter user, you can post updates, follow and view updates from other users, and send a public reply or a private message to connect with another user. It's also a platform for listening. (See chapter 6, Twitter 101, for more information about Twitter.)

Blogs

A *blog* is a type of website that is regularly updated with new content. Blogs are typically maintained by an individual and feature entries that can be personal or professional commentary, descriptions of events, or other material, including graphics or video. Most blogs are interactive, allowing visitors to leave comments. This is what distinguishes a blog from a traditional website.

Your stakeholders might visit a variety of blogs for both information and entertainment, such as the Daily Beast (www.thedailybeast .com), Business Insider (www.businessinsider.com), or TMZ (www .tmz.com). One study shows that over 40 percent of the female population online visits a "mommy blog" for recommendations and advice (Wright & Page, 2009). This phenomenon is big enough to require online versions of the yellow pages where users search among such blog titles for mothers as Hyper Focus Mom (http://hyperfocusmom.blogspot.com), the Parenting Pundit (www .theparentingpundit.com), and Adventures in Tot School (http:// adventuresintotschool.blogspot.com). Education leaders can use blogs to share their thoughts on everything from events happening at their schools to national educational issues. (See chapter 7, Blogging 101, for more information about blogs.)

Blogs can be very powerful. For example, in one small district on the East Coast, after the adoption of a zero tolerance policy, a young student was suspended for bringing a knife to school. Within days, the suspended child's mother had created a blog, started a petition, and contacted the media. She pleaded her case on national television, and respected newspapers covered her story and wrote sympathetic editorials. Within two weeks, the child was reinstated, the suspension was removed from his record, and the school division prepared to revise its guidelines. If the school district had had a blog or used another social media channel, leaders could have put out their side of the story, perhaps changing the outcome or preventing some of the criticism by media outlets.

Message Boards

Internet forums, or *message boards*, are online discussion sites where people converse by posting messages. One *thread* (a string of messages all on one topic) on a community message board sponsored by a local newspaper was started by a mother whose family was soon to move to the area. She posted a message asking where to buy a house to ensure the best school for her child. She was flooded with return messages and opinions, unfiltered by anyone and open for all to read. (Depending on the way they are set up, forums can allow users to be anonymous or require them to register and log in before they can post messages.) Generally, however, you do not have to log in just to read messages. You can lurk to your heart's content.

In their move online, newspapers have sought to bring the community online with them by sponsoring message boards. A popular feature of online news reading is the ability of the reader to post his or her thoughts about a story on the site's message board. Remember the days when a bad news story ended with that day's news cycle? Not anymore. Readers can continue the discussion online with comment threads that can last days and weeks. The more controversial the topic, the more reader responses it will receive.

Most of these forums provide anonymity, which can sometimes result in vitriolic comments or innuendo. Reputable newspapers struggle with the ethics of encouraging a free-for-all environment and balancing it with readers' First Amendment rights. Some host sites establish rules for posting and even monitor comments before posting them.

Micro-News Networks

With many city dailies and some small-town weekly newspapers closing, coverage of local school issues and events has declined. Schools just don't get as many column inches as they used to. Working to fill that void are small online networks for neighborhood news.

Patch (www.patch.com), an AOL company, has spent tens of millions of dollars to build local news sites for communities across the United States. Its goal is for people to "have plenty of opportunities to comment on stories, share [their] opinions, post photos and announcements, and add events to the community calendar" (Patch, 2011). Both Google and Yahoo! are also working to capture a share of this market. By encouraging group participation and citizen journalism, these alternative networks can provide quick access to local news.

School leaders are well advised to cultivate relationships with the reporters and editors from these sites who are assigned to cover education. Get to know them personally, invite them in by providing information about your school, and respond to them promptly when they request additional information. These are critical steps in developing the positive relationships that will work toward fair coverage.

Like message boards, these sites allow anonymous comments, which can plague a school leader. For example, members of one New Jersey community questioned the wisdom of a school building project, maintaining that the money should instead be spent on full-day kindergarten. Luckily, the superintendent was invested in social media. He jumped online, corrected the errors in the postings, and outlined the challenges that school leaders faced in making tough decisions. It's important to let people know that you're paying attention and not willing to let inaccuracies stand.

Who Else Is There?

In their assessment of online media and decisions about social media use, school leaders must consider its connection to traditional media. A national poll conducted in 2010 by Cision and Don Bates of the George Washington University's Master's Degree Program in Strategic Public Relations found that the majority of mainstream journalists now depends on social media for story research. Almost 90 percent of reporters use blogs as sources, 65 percent use social networking sites, and 52 percent use microblogging services, such as Twitter, for information. This is not surprising considering that *digital natives*, those who have not lived in a world without computers, now work on the city desks of most newspapers.

Although the results demonstrate the fast growth of social media as a well-used source of information for mainstream journalists, the good news is that the survey also made it clear that reporters and editors are acutely aware of the need to verify the information they obtain from social media. Eighty-four percent of the journalists surveyed said that social media sources were "slightly less" or "much less" reliable than traditional media, with 49 percent saying social media suffers from a "lack of fact checking, verification and reporting standards" (Cision, 2010).

School-sponsored sites that are actively maintained with transparency serve as a go-to source for reporters who may be tipped off to a story by a community blogger or Twitter feed. For example, a reporter who reads a post on Twitter that after-school sports are about to be eliminated because of budget shortfalls will immediately check the school sites for the truth. A concise, easy-to-understand explanation posted on the web for all to read gives schools an advantage.

Next Steps

1. Identify a recent story about your school division that appeared in local media. What was the online reaction? What strategy could you have used to deal with the response?

2. Where does your school community congregate online? How could you find out?

Key Points

School stakeholders have a presence on the web and on social media sites. They use social media platforms such as Facebook, Twitter, blogs, message boards, and micro-news networks to find and share information and to make their opinions known. Although not regarded as perfect sources of information, reporters go to online networks as *one* source of respected news. Our community already understands that. School leaders would be wise to pay attention.

3 Leading the Change

Research tells us how important strong relationships are to the quality of our life. People in relationships live longer and happier lives. A good marriage makes us stronger; even relationships with our pets make us healthier. It has to do with neuroscience and brain chemicals (Olmert, 2009). Strong relationships matter in our work life as well as our personal life. When Gallup surveys its clients' employees looking for signs of organizational health, it asks them to respond to the statement, "I have a best friend at work" (Leadership Success Interview, 1999). We used to think that if we had friends at home, we didn't need them at work. But as it turns out, we do.

According to researcher and best-selling author Daniel Goleman (1998), "Doing well in our jobs depends to a great or less extent on the work of a web of others." He goes on to say, "Networks of personal contacts are a kind of personal capital" (p. 209). Your network is a source of information and connections. It also gives you social capital and influence. If you think about it, these are many of the same reasons your father joined the Rotary and your mother sat on the library board. Now these networks take on new forms—they are "friends" on Facebook, subscribers to your Twitter feed, visitors to your website, and addresses on your listserv. One of the quickest ways to build a network (for you, your school, or your district) is through social media. So, despite the protests about Facebook by the over-forty crowd, it turns out that he or she who has the most friends *does* win.

To be sure, many of these online friends will—and should—exist in your immediate physical world as well. They'll walk in and out of your office door. You'll see them at meetings and pick up the phone to call them for advice. However, the benefits of a vast network on the Internet are great. The Internet removes such restraints as money, time, and space when creating, cultivating, and continuing social relationships (Anderson & Rainie, 2010). To take advantage of these benefits, leaders must build their networks through social media and then encourage their communities to listen.

Wide Networks, Great Conversations

School leaders have much to bring to the conversation in any community. By virtue of your office, your perspective, and the influence you have on the community's young people, you have the ability to add great value to the public dialogue. Leaders can email, blog, tweet links, and share information and their opinions. Conversations are often prompted by outside events, such as plummeting community and state resources, such headline-grabbing movies as *Waiting for "Superman"* (Chilcotte & Guggenheim, 2010), or the tragedies of student bullying and suicide. School leaders can use their personal and professional networks to great advantage.

Social media allows you to get good information to your stakeholders quickly. It allows you to be transparent and maintain your reputation. When a school or district story gets out of hand, and the newspapers spend fifteen column inches on the details and the six o'clock news leads with your headline, you are at risk of losing ground. Telling the story first through social media networks helps you get the right story out.

Communication through social media tools gives stakeholders reasons to feel emotionally connected to the mission of the school or district and to feel confident in your ability to get the job done. It's about encouraging parents and neighbors to make decisions that support your students. We use social media because it helps us make connections and build community—and building community is about supporting teaching and learning. The beneficiaries of your efforts are your students.

Linking School and Community

School leaders must practice good communication to link school to students' families and communities. This means using the Internet and social media to create robust parent involvement.

A Wallace Foundation study (Louis, Leithwood, Wahlstrom, & Anderson, 2010) of the key components of improved student learning found that "a good deal of evidence supports the popular view that parent involvement has a strong bearing on student achievement" (p. 9). The study goes on to say that "results show that where teachers perceive greater involvement by parents, and where teachers indicate that they practice shared leadership in their schools, student achievement is higher" (p. 9). Educator and author Alan November (2010) concurs:

> The research about the importance of parent
> involvement as a support for student learning
> has been well documented for decades. . . . Yet
> traditional school does not provide enough
> opportunities to link students with their families
> in the midst of hectic everyday schedules. (p. 37)

Despite the fact that they were designed to reach many stakeholders at once, social media tools like email, Twitter, and Facebook feel intimate. When parents hear from school leaders through a Twitter feed or watch a video invitation to an important meeting that's been posted on YouTube, they feel included and they become invested, both in their children's education and in your work as an education leader. When parents become invested in their child's school, everyone wins. As November (2010) states, "In the long run, partnering with the home may be one of the most powerful uses of the Internet" (p. 36).

In addition, through social media networks, parents receive the timely and accurate information they desire and need. As November (2010) goes on to say:

> My children are not the most comprehensive or accurate source of what happens in school, and they are not alone. This lack of accurate information does not breathe life into the parent-school connection. Imagine, instead, a very different parent-child conversation, one where the parent is not at the mercy of what information his or her own child will provide! (pp. 36–37)

Communication—made easier by new technology—builds partnerships both inside and outside the classroom. These partnerships support student learning.

Choking on Facts

In our rush to communicate, however, we must be keenly aware of the types of messages that we provide to stakeholders. School leaders often send messages that are full of information: they want people to know things. For example, consider the following messages that could appear on your school's Twitter feed or Facebook page:

- PTA Arts Festival, Friday, 4–6 pm *[link]*
- Five Teachers Newly Board Certified *[link]*
- Conference Program Now Available Online *[link]*
- Two Longworth Civics Teachers on Channel 9 Tonight to Discuss the New Textbook *[link]*

These are important messages—all good news and worth sharing—and we feel pressure to get the good news out. Leaders want to tell their stakeholders what is going on in their schools and where to get more information. These messages also reassure our stakeholders that things are going well; in other words, that their children are being well taught and well tended.

But there should be more to our communication than simply providing information and reassurance. Instead of just pouring out facts, we must also engage our stakeholders by asking their opinions, arousing their curiosity, directing their efforts, and helping to inform their decisions concerning their children's education. Parents are asking for a new kind of conversation.

In his book *How We Decide*, journalist and author Jonah Lehrer (2009) explores current research on the workings of the human brain. He notes how, over time, we have come to define ourselves as human by our rationality: "There is only one problem with this assumption of human rationality," Lehrer says. "It's wrong" (p. xv). He continues:

> The mind is composed of a messy network of different areas many of which are involved with the production of emotion. Whenever someone makes a decision [such as whether to send their child to public or private school] the brain is awash in feeling, driven by its inexplicable passions. Even when a person tries to be reasonable and restrained, these emotional impulses secretly influence judgment. (p. xv)

The research that he reports has huge implications for educators and education leaders. He demonstrates that we all badly misjudge what it takes to make a decision. Despite what we think, when we make decisions, we are not just using facts and figures. We are also strongly influenced by our emotions. When we don't take these emotions into account, we often make bad decisions.

In education, this also means that we often fail in our communications with our parents and community because we send messages only to our stakeholders' left brains—their analytic side. We neglect the right side of the brain—the emotional side. According to Lehrer

(2009), "Good decisions require us to use both sides of the mind" (p. xvi). We cannot make decisions without our emotions.

If we are going to help parents make good decisions about their children's education—decisions about course work, discipline, classroom support, careers, and postsecondary education—and encourage the community around us to make good decisions about supporting their schools, we have to feed both the left and the right brain with strong messages. We can't just send out facts, announcements, and test scores to the left brain. We have to also send out messages that make parents feel included and help them to understand which of the decisions they are making are the most important.

This is often difficult for educators; we take the training of the rational mind seriously. "None of that softer stuff," we say. "Just give us the facts. It's clear, rational decisions that get us where we need to go." When we feel pressed to get the information out, what appeals to the emotions—the "softer stuff"—gets left by the wayside. It takes more time, and, we reason, it's not that important anyway.

Social media has the unique ability to appeal to the emotional brain—to reach the softer side. It can convey information in a way that also makes us feel like part of a community, engages people who might not otherwise pay attention, taps into stakeholders' creativity and curiosity, and builds lasting relationships in ways that facts, figures, press releases, and newsletters cannot.

We started this chapter with some examples of information-based headlines. Now here are some relationship-building messages tailor-made for a Facebook page, a Tweet, or a text message:

- Love science? Help us judge the science fair! *[link]*
- How are we doing with the new school lunch program? Let us know. *[link]*
- Help your kid! Check out the new elementary parent reading toolkit. *[link]*
- Fun & fitness! Lamott High School gym, Saturday, 9a.m.–4p.m. Learn new skills. *[link]*

In each case, you are sending information, but you are also invit-ing your stakeholders to be engaged in the process. They can follow the links you provide in your message to fill out the survey or sign on to be a judge or learn how to help their child read. This type of communication goes beyond communicating information—it offers stakeholders a chance to *do* something. It builds community.

Soft Selling in a Hard Market

Social media is also a great customer service tool for school lead-ers. Valarie Zeithaml (Zeithaml & Bitner, 1996), internationally recognized author and service marketing professor at Kenan-Flagler Business School at the University of North Carolina, says that our brains gather a great deal of information beyond what is available to our rational minds. Her research demonstrates how influential what she calls "the intangibles" of an organization can be in the opinions our stakeholders have of us. How our parents feel when they walk in the door of our school or office can be a huge determinant in whether they think we are doing a good job. They might ask such things as, "Are the halls clean? Is it easy to find the front office? Did people greet me warmly?"

Educators have a tendency to stand behind their desks and offer test scores as evidence of competency because they think that's what matters most to stakeholders and taxpayers; however, test scores are not the only thing parents and other members of the community want from us. Our stakeholders are looking for signs that we respect them and want to collaborate with them. Being available and visible on Facebook, Twitter, and YouTube can be an intangible for a school or district. If we offer the right intangibles, our stakeholders give us points for our transparency, and they are more apt to get involved. Social media can help us communicate our respect and desire to collaborate and partner in ways that publications, PowerPoint pre-sentations, and letters sent home in students' backpacks cannot.

Five Ways to Reconnect With Stakeholders in the 21st Century

Here are some great ways to reframe your communication efforts:

1. **Stop sending messages.** Invite your stakeholders into a conversation instead. Provide time or space for stakeholders to get involved.

2. **Don't always tell people what you want them to know.** Instead, give them the information *they* want to have. Sometimes, this information falls in the category of "what's in it for me" or "what's in it for my children." (For instance, "Here's a list of names and email addresses of parents of children who participated in the program last year. They've agreed to talk with prospective parents who might have questions.") It's a place to start building stronger relationships.

3. **Start asking stakeholders what they want and need to know, what services would be useful, and whom they would like to hear from, and once you ask, use their answers.** This strategy includes your stakeholders in the mission. (Don't be the kind of district that makes a big deal about asking, but then stores the answers on the shelf.)

4. **Build a sustainable communication effort.** Communication is a process, not a product. It takes time. It is a job that's never done. You have to plan for the long run. Connect stakeholders with their peers. Let them add to the conversation.

5. **Create a climate where everyone in the organization feels a shared responsibility for creating relationships and building trust with stakeholders.** Communication is not just the job of the communications department. To have everyone on board means that employees need to feel included in the mission of the organization. That takes work too. Although the tone is set from the top, a climate of collaboration spreads from staff members to parents and ultimately gets the job done.

Next Steps

1. For one week, collect copies of all the communication your school or district sends to its parents: newsletters, backpack letters, push email, web posts, robocalls (automated calls), Tweets, and Facebook posts. How many of the messages contained information that the school or district wanted parents to know? How many messages sought to build relationships? How many offered a way for parents to respond?

2. Identify a single issue that needs more communication (for example, a boundary change, new curriculum information, or new health department regulations). Make note of the means of communication you have used so far, what's working, and what's not. What messages have you sent thus far? Keep these notes.

Creating Change in the Trenches

Change is always a process. It happens over time. We have watched many superintendents and principals engage their communities in change, none more successfully than our friend Steve.

Steve is a well-liked veteran elementary principal who leads a school with a strong academic reputation and an active parent community. He came to the school two-and-a-half years ago, determined to bring the school's use of technology into the 21st century. In the classroom, that meant, among other things, that students would create web pages with links and videos based on their online research, have conversations with other students around the world, and have the opportunity to participate in a weekly, after-school writing club that would publish student work online. Students would even have access to ebooks for their own reading pleasure.

Right from the start, Steve began to use the new technologies to actively engage his parents—including creating an email newsletter, a Gmail account for parents to use for reporting absences and pick-up/drop-off changes, parent access to a systemwide software network that allows parents to see student assignments and school calendars, and a sophisticated emergency response system. The school even began setting up Twitter accounts.

You might think these changes would be readily accepted in an educated community such as the one in which Steve worked. But, as it turned out, Steve's school was a classic textbook case for change: there were early adopters, the great mass in the middle, and the foot draggers. In the beginning, Steve reported that some parents regularly called the office asking to have a paper copy of the newsletter sent to them. "I just told them no," Steve said. "I was not going to reward bad behavior."

It took the school nearly a year to get all the families to register an email account for the newsletter and for the emergency and messaging system. Steve recalls the day that everyone was on board as a red-letter day. But, Steve says, the coaching continues:

> We have to train new parents—especially on how to access the online website that has student assignments and calendars. People forget their passwords, and some need reminders on how to navigate the site. We hold trainings at PTO meetings and sometimes we keep the lab open for parent use. We make ourselves available to help.
>
> Each year, I send a letter home by snail mail at the beginning of the year, with instructions on how to access the information they want on the web. But after that, I post the class lists and everything else online. They have to go get it.

What are the benefits for all this work? For the staff, Steve sees a reduction in the nuisance work of running a school, including fewer calls to the front office, fewer homework questions, and a huge reduction in the paper budget. Steve explains further:

> Starting out, some of the teachers saw this as just another thing to do—but now they see that parents aren't bugging them so much. It's actually made their job easier.

> We are careful to do any teacher training
> on the new tools and software during their
> planning time or embedded in the workday
> by hiring substitutes for the classroom. I think
> it's important to demonstrate your respect for
> teachers' time and treat them like professionals.

Parents have become huge supporters of the effort. They see pictures of school events and field trips and have access to their children's work online. They can find school information any time, day or night, and Steve takes care to create opportunities for parents to reflect on what's going on and ask questions. "I work to put out a regular and consistent message in my own voice," he says. "It has raised the trust factor enormously."

At the end of the process, Steve reflected on the additional benefits:

> I am amazed at how much easier it is to build
> consensus at the school now. With more
> information and more connection to the school,
> people are more willing to trust that you will
> make decisions that are in the best interest of
> their children. We have become a much more
> collaborative organization.

Strategies With Solid Results

When introducing the new technologies and use of social media to both his students and all the adults in the school community, Steve employed the following communication strategies:

- **You have to listen first.** The most critical message about parents today is that they expect to be included. They want you to know what they think and to give it serious consideration as you lead the school or district. They want you to listen. All along the way, Steve worked with his parent leaders. They were clear with him from the beginning about their expectations, and he was equally clear about his. The honest conversation worked.

- **Your employees must be your first customers.** Confident, respected employees help you create change. They encourage students and parents alike. Some staff members may be reluctant at first to use new tools, but you will never successfully transform your school classrooms if your staff are not on board. Once your staff are on board, they are your largest and most effective sales force. You are changing your school culture, and you must manage that change—not just teach people how to use new software. Steve is a principal who is quick to give credit to his staff for their work. When he came to the school, he immediately sought out the technologically savvy staff members and supported their efforts. He made technology cool.

- **You need to segment your audiences, because each group will want different information and support.** Steve is very judicious about the messages he sends. He recognizes that his messages carry more weight, and he gains more respect when he doesn't overload anyone's mailbox. In our hurry to provide information, we often don't pay enough attention to the needs of our individual stakeholder groups. Remember taxpayers in your community want to know you are using their tax dollars well; your parents want to know that their children are safe, nurtured, and learning well; and the business community wants to know that you are teaching the next generation of workers the skills that they need to be successful. Sometimes these interests overlap, but not always. (And none of these groups are particularly interested in the details of your latest internal reorganization. That's a message you should save for your school board or city council.) Inundating everyone with all your messages just turns off your supporters.

- **Customer service goes a long way.** This is a classic message that is still important today. We already know that people will judge the work you do by what they see and experience—how well served they feel. How creative are your bulletin boards? How cheerful is the front office staff? Is the lawn mowed? Now there is a new place to be seen and served. Is your school or district doing a good job reaching out to its stakeholders using the web and social media? If you are, they will reason, then you must be doing a good job with the students as well.

- **Repeat your important messages often.** Have you noticed that sometimes a commercial repeats several times during the same television program? That's not a mistake. It's probably an intentional move to ingrain the message in our heads. The more people hear a message, the more they are apt to remember and believe it. Make your news available everywhere. Don't make it hard to find. Surely you have had the experience of going to a website and not being able to find an event date, a telephone number, or an employee title. It's frustrating. Don't risk losing your audience because they can't find the information they need.

- **Give yourself permission to fail.** Not everything you try will work. Not long ago, a group of our colleagues—separated by distance but all interested in new ways of communication—decided to set up a private wiki site where they could exchange ideas as they worked. They envisioned the website as an easy way to stay in touch and share useful information with friends. They gave themselves three months to try it out, but by the fourth week, the site went dormant, never to be revived again. There were many reasons why. Among other things, the software turned out to be cumbersome and the process somehow didn't fit with the group members' individual work rhythms. So they let it go. Tools will come and go (remember the Edsel?), and some tools will fit your needs better than others. You have to experiment. You have to play.

- **Use all the tools at your disposal.** You have to repeat your messages and experiment to find which form of media works best for each stakeholder group and type of message. Maybe budget messages work best with emails and a website because these messages require thoughtful consideration. On the other hand, a call for volunteers might be more effective delivered face to face, in meetings, and via Twitter. Be clever. Think outside of the box.

Next Steps

1. Gather a small group of parents or teachers (or parents *and* teachers) to talk about communication in your school or district. What do they like and dislike?

2. Using the information you've already gathered in your survey and gleaned from your personal reflections, discuss with the group ways that you might reach key stakeholder groups more effectively. Identify goals for the new communication effort.

Key Points

Social media is designed to help us build partnerships and keep people connected to the school and district. In schools, we often get too busy sending out information. Research demonstrates that to make good decisions our brains use both *information* and *emotion*. We need to engage our stakeholders' creativity and curiosity—as well as give them facts and figures—if they are to make good decisions on behalf of their children and feel they are a part of the community.

Moving your community toward consistently using new media is like leading any kind of change: you have to listen to your customers first and include them in your planning. You must keep reminding them of the vision you created together, train them repeatedly, offer them support, use all the tools at your disposal, and not be afraid to fail.

4

Planning Your Debut and Creating an Online Platform

When we interviewed one superintendent about his district's use of social media, he insisted that he ignored the message boards and blogs: "I don't have time for that," he said. However, the more we talked, the more we saw how social media had already affected his job:

- He had withdrawn a contract offered to a new teacher after he was alerted to a particular online conversation on the teacher's Facebook page. By sharing intimate details of his partying habits and views toward women, the candidate had revealed a side of himself that would not be a good fit with the school community.

- A newly elected school board member conducted her campaign using social media.

- Parents at a recent school board meeting shared results from an online survey they conducted regarding a school closing.

In fact, he did have firsthand experience with social media; he avoided what might have been a bad personnel decision and he learned how the medium can be used to persuade an audience. Even rural communities, such as the one this superintendent leads, are not immune to the influence of social media. Indeed, even if you think you are not involved in the conversation, social media has probably already affected your life more than you realize. Its presence in all our lives underscores the importance for leaders to consider how they can use social media as a tool to benefit their leadership.

In many school districts, changing the way you communicate with your stakeholders represents a sea change. It will not happen just by firing up a Twitter account. To make a sustainable change, you will have to:

- Really want to engage your stakeholders in a two-way dialogue.
- Listen to what other people are saying.
- Be willing to learn.
- Write in an accessible way.
- Market your schools and their successes.
- Answer tough questions.
- Be available.
- Be a new kind of leader.

Checking Your Culture

A close examination of your school, district, and community culture will give you clues about where to start.

Assess yourself using the following checklist. Indicate whether you strongly agree, agree, somewhat agree, or don't agree with each statement.

1. Personal attributes
   a. We're comfortable using technology.
   b. We're willing to take the time to learn what we don't know.
   c. We acknowledge the benefits of social media.
   d. We are willing to take the time required to listen and to respond to comments.

e. We can learn how to respond to uncomplimentary comments.

f. We know how to write effective stories.

g. We're able to draw the fine line between putting ourselves out there and maintaining a professional demeanor.

h. We view ourselves as having an open-door policy.

i. We are willing to take some risks.

2. Current communication efforts

a. We regularly communicate with local media by issuing press releases and by responding to information requests.

b. We publish a regular newsletter.

c. We have an active website.

d. We are effective at communicating by email.

e. The majority of our community is online.

f. Our community values communication from the school.

g. We regularly meet with the community and parent groups.

h. We have conducted customer service surveys of our parents.

The results of this survey help to identify your areas of strength and those where you need further study and work. For example, if your current communication efforts do not include an active website, that is where your work may need to begin. Not willing to take risks with your communication? If so, then using social media at this time may not be a good fit. Whatever the results, take time to review them as an indication of your current school communication program. The results may also provide a map of where to go next.

Collaborative Effort

After your assessment, gather some trusted staff members and parent leaders to lead the charge. Perhaps your school's public relations director can head up a team, or perhaps some staff members are eager to pilot a small social media effort directed at a particularly active issue or community on behalf of the school or district. For example, younger staff members could use an internal social networking tool to share ideas with each other. A school leader could develop a blog for the parent community. An instructional leader could set up a Facebook page covering a particular issue currently facing the community. Starting with efforts like these and then evaluating their success set the stage for more. How will you know if you've been successful? You might decide that if you get 5 percent of your community on your Facebook page in three months, then you've achieved success. If you don't reach that goal, what will you do? You might then devise a plan to drive people to your page. Remember, your efforts are a work in progress and where you start is not as important as *that* you start.

Eventually, you will build a system of communication using different platforms in social media. No one technology should be used in isolation; rather, each communication platform should serve as one of the tools that make up your school's or district's social media toolkit. However, you have to start somewhere, so take small steps as you gain experience.

Remembering Your Goals

Social media is an opportunity to broaden and strengthen the connection between home and school. Electronic gradebooks, telephone messaging systems, and email have already changed the landscape, making well-managed information delivery more efficient, faster, and more cost-effective. Social media expands that capability and allows leaders to connect without any filters and to engage more members of the community by bypassing the barriers of time and space.

The public wants to know that those taking care of the community's children are genuine, committed, and competent. They also want to know them as human beings. Social media provides an outlet for "straight from the heart" communication. You are on your way.

Next Steps

1. Ask members of your leadership team what social media sites they use. What are the benefits and limitations of each?

2. Name a recent change your school made in which you sought community feedback. Could you have used social media to collect that feedback? Why or why not?

Your Online Platform

Social media and traditional media are not mutually exclusive. In fact, we must move away from *replacement* thinking, and focus instead on *complementary* thinking. Look for ways that social media can leverage your current communication methods and vice versa. Think of them as partners to the traditional methods: meetings, focus groups, and even the printed newsletter. A combined communication platform—one that utilizes both new technologies and traditional methods—expands your reach. Remember—not everyone gets news in the same ways. You must appeal to a broad range of stakeholders. The centerpiece for all these efforts should be the school's website.

Your Website

Think of your website as the home base for your school information platform. Figure 4.1 (page 50) shows the website as the centerpiece of a communication network. Your community will go to your website to find information. Your website's focus should be on service, and its product is information. Deliver it with ease and polish, and you will develop loyal customers.

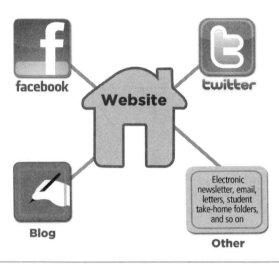

Figure 4.1: The website as the centerpiece of a school's communication system.

Older school websites were set up to serve the district's needs for information. Newer school websites have evolved, however, to place greater emphasis on meeting the user's needs and framing things from the user's point of view. If you're a parent, you're directed to a page designed specifically to provide information relevant to you. If you are a staff member or a member of the media, you follow separate links to get to different customized information.

An essential step in moving your digital communication forward is tracking your users and evaluating your website. Many elements combine to make an effective website, including ease of use, relevance, consistency, and regular updates.

Tracking Your Users and Getting Feedback

When developing your website, it is helpful to track your users. Where are they going on your website? What are they looking for? Google Analytics (www.google.com/analytics) is a free service you can use to gather a wealth of data about your online presence. Do you want to know how many people visited your site on April 4? You'll find the number using Google Analytics, along with much more information, such as the average amount of time a visitor spends on your site, the percentage of new visitors each month, and how people get to your site. With all this data available, you need to figure out what's relevant to you and your particular situation. What are your communication goals? How can your website meet them?

One school board we know charged the superintendent with the task of increasing the district's engagement with the people in their community. She devised a plan that included digital communication and set about to increase the number of visitors to the school district's website. She put together a team, which included PTA representatives and some outside help from the school district's communication office. They studied the site and made a list of three things that would immediately boost traffic:

1. Update the home page daily (with a picture, notice, video, or link) to show that this is an active source of information.

2. Advertise the presence of the site prominently in all school publications.

3. Create a school Facebook page to drive traffic to the website, and broadcast the district's daily updates on Facebook as well. From conversations with parents, she knew her school community was active on Facebook. Establishing a school page allowed her to meet her community where they were and reach many members of the community.

Within thirty days, the superintendent had doubled their website traffic.

Next, she took on the challenge of sustaining the web effort and improving the page's organization and content. She saw this as long-term work and decided to include a *site audit*—an analysis of a site's usability from the perspective of users.

You may want to employ this tactic in your district too. Perhaps you can ask your technology or communications staff for help. Start the site audit by asking web users to take a survey (electronic surveys are inexpensive and easy to administer) around the following categories:

- **Navigation and functionality**—What sorts of information do you usually seek on the site? How easy is it to find what you're looking for? How easy is it to locate the answers to frequently asked questions? How helpful are the answers?

- **User control**—How does the page size appear on different screen sizes and with different browsers?

- **Language and content**—How prominent is the important information? Is the language easy to understand, or does it contain too much jargon?

It's possible that your users will advise you to ditch the site and begin again, but it's more likely that making some simple changes, based on your stakeholders' answers, will make a big improvement. If you satisfy your users' basic needs, your website will get more traffic and communication will be more effective.

Outposts

The *outposts* are the social media websites outside of your school website where you can maintain an online presence. At these outposts schools interact with stakeholders and guide them back to the home base (that is, the school website). This is what our superintendent did in the example cited earlier in this chapter. At this writing, the three most popular outposts are Twitter, Facebook, and blogs.

- **Twitter** (http://twitter.com) is the quickest-paced social media platform. It can provide an immediate touch point with your community. Brevity is the name of the game on Twitter, because Twitter messages, called *Tweets*, are limited to 140 characters (although there is an option to increase if needed). This outpost is very conversational with users providing information, commentary, and resources. Users can access and send messages while on the go via their mobile devices. Like all social media channels, the user needs to be prepared to participate by sending Tweets to followers and commenting on their responses. (See chapter 6, Twitter 101, for more detailed information about this platform.)

- **Facebook** (www.facebook.com), with 800 million users, is the largest social network, and it continues to grow. The atmosphere is one of sharing in a casual environment. Facebook requires the *authentication* of its users, which means there's no room for anonymity. This is a plus for a school environment. Another plus is Facebook's ability to spread information: a post on your Facebook *wall* (the place where what you write appears on your Facebook page) automatically appears on the home page of all your *friends* (those who have signed on to view your page). So, in turn, all the friends of friends see the news as well. With no email lists to maintain, Facebook is an attractive communication solution for budget-strapped schools. (See chapter 5, Facebook 101, for more detailed information about this platform.)

- **Blogs,** one of the first social media platforms, are written by individuals or organizations, and give the writer the opportunity to offer information and opinions about important subjects and provide the community with a space in which to react. They can be likened to online journals. Blogs need not be limited to text; they can include photos, audio, and video in any combination. Done well—that is, updated regularly and made relevant to readers' needs—a blog can be a solid link to the community. (See chapter 7, Blogging 101, for more detailed information about this platform.)

Each time you add a social media outpost to your communication toolbox, use your traditional media outlets to broadcast the news. Create and display posters with your Facebook page and include information about your Twitter feed in the school or district newsletter. Hand out paper copies of your first blog post with its address (the URL) at Back-to-School night. Each time you add an outpost to your toolbox, integrate your new channels with your traditional ones to add dimension to your communication process. Start with what you post on your website, and then use all your outposts (digital and traditional) to let people know what's there. By doing so, you will expand both the conversation and the number of participants.

Next Steps

1. Identify two or three school district websites that catch your attention. What are the qualities that make them effective?

2. Looking at these websites, list the social media channels they note on their home pages.

Key Points

Social media is a particularly good medium to communicate authentically and to bring a community together around your leadership. It offers "straight from the horse's mouth" information without interpretation. Gather staff members and parent leaders around you, assess where your community is, and decide where you want to begin. Start small, and go from there.

Integrating your new channels with your traditional ones is essential to making the communication process efficient. Your website is the centerpiece of your web presence. Develop that first, and then use your outposts to drive stakeholders to your website. Thus, you expand both the conversation and the number of participants who participate.

5 Facebook 101

We often speak with school and district leaders who say they are frightened to death of Facebook. Media headlines about "Facebook run amok" can turn a leader's wise caution into an unreasonable fear, resulting in school boards and superintendents adopting policies that prohibit Facebook use altogether. As we write, for example, a Missouri law to prevent teacher contact with students via Facebook is being challenged in court. A clear understanding of Facebook, and all social media platforms for that matter, is important to address the risks responsibly before stepping into the social media world where your communities are talking.

Profiles Versus Pages

The basis of many Facebook horror stories comes from the use (and misuse) of Facebook profiles. A *profile* is a collection of information within a Facebook page where individuals can make personal information—such as education and work, personal philosophy, favorite arts and entertainment, and so on—available for a select group of friends, yet restrict it from public view (or not). For example, a newly hired superintendent was fired for posting what he thought was a humorous update on his Facebook profile, which he had made public. The remark was deemed inappropriate by his school board, and he was toast.

There's a difference, however, between an individual profile and a Facebook business page. *Profiles* are for individuals, and *pages* are for businesses and organizations. School districts should create a page, not a profile. Certain features are not permitted on pages but are permitted on profiles, and vice versa. For example, users can "like" (previously referred to as "fan") the page of a business they like, whereas users "friend" the profiles of their friends and acquaintances. Pages have a more formal quality than profiles, and because of that, users approach pages with different expectations. Many users come to an organizational page with the willingness to accept the established guidelines and an understanding that things are not as personal as on a profile. However, common to all Facebook experiences is the expectation that the experience will be interactive and that they will have the ability to leave feedback.

Terms to Know

There are four important Facebook terms that you'll need to know as you become familiar with this social media platform: *wall, news feed, like,* and *comment.*

Wall

The *wall* is a space on your Facebook page where you, as the Facebook administrator, can post items of interest for your community. You can also allow your users to post updates to your wall. (We discuss this later in the chapter.)

For example, Godfrey-Lee Public Schools in Wyoming, Michigan, posted an update on their wall congratulating a member of the girls' basketball team for being chosen as an all-state honorable mention. Each post on a wall shows the time of the posting along with buttons a user can click to "like" or add their own comment to the post.

News Feed

The *news feed*—the center column of an individual profile—is a constantly updating list of stories from the profiles and pages that the user follows on Facebook. Even though this feature is not part of a business page, understanding how the news feed works will help you to understand the way your news items will appear on your users' news feeds. When users interact with your page, their interaction shows up on all their friends' news feeds, further spreading your message.

Like

Like is a way for the person reading your page to give positive feedback and to connect with things he or she cares about on Facebook. A user can "like" a post or "like" the entire page. When a user clicks the "like" button on your site, a notice will appear in the "top news" or "recent news" feeds of each of his or her friends with a link back to your page. Thus, if your post receives twenty "likes" the result is that your message is forwarded to the friend networks of twenty additional users. This outcome is one of the viral benefits of Facebook—your message gets out to a broader audience.

Comment

The *comments box* is a space where users can remark on your posts. In the example from Godfrey-Lee Public Schools, several people commented on the post about the girls' basketball player who was congratulated for her accomplishment, including one teacher who commented that she knew the student was destined for greatness when she had her in the sixth grade. When these users commented on the post, it automatically appeared on their friends' news feeds as well.

Next Steps

1. View three school Facebook sites. Identify the wall, the comments, and the likes. What similarities and differences can you detect in each school's approach?

2. What has been your experience with Facebook? What particular audiences in your school community might find it useful?

Taking Charge of Your Facebook Community

Unlike traditional, one-way forms of school communication, such as newsletters or memos, the Facebook format encourages the community to engage with the school or district by providing a digital platform for discussion and feedback. Facebook provides a rich opportunity for community and school to engage with each other. School-leaders-turned-Facebook-page-administrators can direct a positive flow of Facebook content in three important ways:

1. Managing privacy settings

2. Monitoring comments

3. Maintaining strong, active leadership of their Facebook community

Managing Privacy Settings

It only takes a few minutes to create a Facebook page (www .facebook.com/pages/create.php) using the default settings (Facebook, 2011). A quick start, however, means giving up the ability to adjust the privacy settings beyond the default settings Facebook deems necessary to provide adequate security. The page set-up process is where you control the degree of access you will allow your readers and the degree to which they can post feedback. You can modify your settings at any point to increase or reduce your level of privacy.

The *most restrictive approach* to privacy will prohibit users from posting any feedback at all. Although this gives your school or district complete control of the content, it defeats the purpose of using Facebook as a two-way communication platform. Yes, you get your message out on a different platform, but you eliminate the option for users to respond. Facebook provides the virtual space to talk with your broader community in a way that meetings at school do not. It brings in a larger audience, and it should give everyone an equal opportunity to engage.

A *less restrictive approach* to privacy allows readers to comment only on items you've posted. To do this, you set your privacy settings to allow those who "like" your page to comment. (When someone has "liked" your page, his or her authentication information—including his or her name and Facebook profile page—is available for you to see.) Our informal survey of about one hundred school Facebook pages in the United States shows that allowing readers to comment on your posts is the most common approach. Here is an example of a school posting: "March is Youth Art Month. Here is a sampling of student art from several schools." (The post would feature pictures of the artwork or links to the artwork.) Many readers might signal that they "liked" the post, and several might add comments, such as: "Wow, our students are talented!" and "I can't wait to see more!"

This is a common type of exchange between Facebook users and a school. Postings of a congratulatory nature commonly are met with strong shows of community loyalty and support.

A second kind of comment exchange is when users ask questions. For example, a post about class ring orders on one school's page resulted in a community member—an alumni of the school—posting to ask if she could still get a ring from her graduation year. Indeed, she could, and the school Facebook administrator posted the number to call to get more information. Notice the customer service aspect of this exchange with the responsiveness of the school (giving follow-up information) and the delight of the customer. This is another benefit of Facebook.

The *least restrictive approach* to feedback is to allow those who "like" your page to post to your wall. Anyone coming to your page who has "liked" it can create his or her own post and have it appear in equal display to the school post. Salem-Keizer Public Schools in Oregon provides this kind of open access that encourages users to post questions and concerns and allows the school a chance to respond. One post on the Salem-Kaizer wall was from a parent who said she was discouraged by crowded classrooms and asked about plans for reducing class size. Within the hour, the school responded, answering her question and providing information about the implications of their budget shortfall.

This example demonstrates some of the benefits to providing open access to your page, and we believe this kind of exchange is the ultimate goal. Nevertheless, we've spoken to several school leaders who initially set up their Facebook pages to allow wall posts, only to remove the privilege after users bombarded the page with inappropriate wall posts after disagreements about controversial issues (in one case it was an early school closing necessitated by inclement weather). Schools that allow full privileges in a least restrictive environment must monitor their pages closely and immediately remove inappropriate wall posts.

Monitoring Comments

The Facebook page administrator, the individual who posts and monitors your page content, can hide comments and wall posts. Establishing and publicizing consistent guidelines for how items will be hidden is important. Most administrators do not hide comments such as "I don't like the new plan for kindergarten orientation" simply for being negative. Hiding critical comments violates open discussion and calls into question the transparency of the school or district. Hiding comments that are defamatory or lewd, or violate an individual's privacy, however, is well within the guidelines of acceptable use.

Many Facebook administrators find members of their Facebook community will challenge negative comments by other users. Nicole Kirby, the administrator of Missouri's Park Hill School District Facebook page, has found this to be true (personal communication, March 2011). When the school year in her district was extended because of snow days, many parents took their grumbling to the district's Facebook page. But other parents defended the district by posting such comments as, "They did what was best for the kids!" Experienced Facebook users generally agree that negative comments (unless well founded) will be overcome by a flood of positive support from the community.

Maintaining Strong, Active Leadership

Facebook administrators need to take strong leadership of their Facebook communities to manage a successful page. Others in the organization may be allowed to post as well, but it's important to designate one person as the host. (Remember that there is no way to limit access to anyone who has been given permission to post—it's all or nothing.)

As host, the administrator creates a space and sets the tone for discussion. Nicole Kirby, the Park Hill administrator, has posted a valuable set of guidelines on Park Hill's site that spell out clearly what's allowed and what won't be tolerated on the page (Park Hill School District, n.d.). The guidelines clarify that postings by visitors do not reflect the opinions of the school district, instruct people to be respectful and engage in civil discussion, and spell out the kind of comments that the school reserves the right to remove.

As a school leader, your job is to help your community envision what the Facebook community can accomplish for your school or district and then target content and discussion items to turn the vision into reality. Post content on your page to do the following:

- Educate
  - Introduce new staff members.
  - Provide event reminders.
  - Give details about policy decisions.
- Entertain
  - Post pictures and videos.
  - Showcase student achievement and awards.
  - Update with scores from student sporting events.
- Engage
  - Conduct a poll on lighthearted or serious topics.
  - Ask for nominations for awards.
  - Provide opportunities for input on policy discussions.

Looking at other school pages as well as pages from other organizations will help you generate ideas for content. It's also important to decide how often you'll post. Kirby says that she's judicious about what she posts, not wanting to saturate her audience with too many messages.

The following list will help you identify and manage critical issues to publish a successful Facebook page.

- Behind the Scenes
  - Assign a community manager.
  - Give update rights to other administrators.
  - Create guidelines.
  - Check the page frequently.
  - Define targets for success.
- Engagement Tactics
  - Post regularly.
  - Keep posts informal.
  - Ask questions of your stakeholders.

- ◆ Give shout-outs to fans.
- ◆ Respond to posts.
- ◆ Keep updates short.
- ◆ Get your readers' attention.
- • Promotion
  - ◆ Alert your community about your page offline.
  - ◆ Link from other platforms.
  - ◆ Add a link to your email signature.
  - ◆ "Like," comment on, share, and email your own feeds.

Use Facebook to announce school events. Post notices of important meetings. Refer your readers to interesting articles or stories about education on the web. Provide links to your website whenever you can. Use Facebook to drive traffic to your website where you have stored additional valuable information. Above all, ask your readers questions. Engage them in an ongoing discussion about their children and their children's education. Use Facebook to foster a new kind of conversation.

Next Steps

1. Review three school or district Facebook pages, and identify the privacy settings applied. Are users allowed to post to the wall, post comments, or not post at all?

2. Look at three business Facebook pages. Describe who their audience is and how they attempt to engage them. What can you tell about their privacy settings?

Key Points

The benefits of establishing a Facebook presence for your school community, both in expanding your audience and in providing a platform for meaningful conversation, are hard to ignore. With a good understanding of the risks, start with small steps and apply some common sense to develop a page that will meet the objectives of your school's communication plan.

Virtual communities are similar to actual communities in that they both flourish under strong leadership. You have more control online than you think, both in setting social expectations and in moderating the discussion. Your job is to create a place where people will find it worth their time to join in conversation.

6 Twitter 101

Superintendent David Britten of Godfrey-Lee Public Schools in Wyoming, Michigan was like many users who set up a Twitter account (http://twitter.com) but initially don't do much with it. However, when he noticed what other educators were doing, he jumped in and now doesn't go a single day without tweeting. "Once you've actually experienced the value, you'll start to see the point," he says (D. Britten, personal communication, November 2010).

Superintendent Pam Moran of Albemarle County Public Schools in Albemarle County, Virginia, has been finding and sharing resources on Twitter since 2008, enriching her district's professional development in content, pedagogy, and technology. She says she tweets to "link to staff and learners across boundaries of district, state, and nation to celebrate successes and shoulder failures" (P. Moran, personal communication, November 2010).

Twitter often serves as a first step in creating fruitful professional connections. Moran's Tweets about learning environments have resulted in a connection to an instructor at Michigan State, which turned into a Skype session with her principals. Several of them made further connections with the instructor, which resulted in further onsite professional development. Moran says, "I don't use it to tell people what I've had for dinner. I don't share that kind of information." Instead, she creates conversation around professional topics, such as technology use in instructional delivery, she offers nuggets of wisdom from conferences she attends, and she provides links to other interesting posts. Her Twitter experiences have led her to participate in "webinars on Skype, in Google Docs, and on the phone with some amazing educators who I otherwise would not have had a chance to know."

The Benefits of Brevity and Speed

Part of Twitter's appeal is the limited message size. Allowing just 140 characters (including spaces between words) forces writers to choose their words carefully. Reminiscent of the telegram where words cost money, forced brevity results in messages that are succinct and concise.

This brevity is perfect for your stakeholders, who, as we've stated already, want their news and information in real time. They want news that is accurate, useful, and geared to their needs, and they want it right away—in the palms of their hands. In schools, news and information are about students, and it makes parents' busy lives less complicated when they are easy to read and understand. Twitter is made for the current generation of parents.

Twitter Shorthand

The brevity of Twitter messages, referred to as *Tweets*, necessitates a type of shorthand to make the most of the 140-character limit. Following are some examples of Twitter shorthand.

- **@username:** Twitter users have usernames that begin with the @ symbol, which work as a tool for conversation. Writers use the @ symbol to respond to or mention other Twitter users. For example, a user might write, "Check out @AASADan for ESEA updates."

- **URL shorteners:** URL shorteners are essential for Twitter users. Our favorite is the Google URL shortener (http://goo.gl).

This tool will convert a long URL to a tiny version of the same link, thus taking up fewer characters of the 140 limit.

- **#hashtag:** Using the # symbol before a keyword creates a *hashtag*, a useful tool to group all Tweets on a similar topic. For example, a school leader creates the hashtag "#Mt.View budget" and includes it in all Tweets relevant to budget discussions. Here's what a Tweet would look like: "Give input tonight at 7 at Mt. View HS on #Mt.View budget." A Twitter search for "#Mt. View budget" would result in all the Tweets on that topic grouped together.

- **RT@username:** *RT* means "retweet." When you like what someone else has tweeted and you want to share it with your followers, you RT it and the message is sent. This is what it looks like: "RT@AASAMeg: Lessons learned when lightning strikes twice. Goo.gl/cgMXC"

- **DM@username:** A *DM*—direct message—is a way to have a private conversation via Twitter with anyone who is following you. A Tweet starting with DM goes only to one person rather than your entire network of followers.

What's in It for Me?

Twitter can be particularly useful to school leaders in several ways.

1. You can *listen* to what other people are saying to:
   - Learn what's important to your parents.
   - Listen to community members' concerns.

2. You can segment your audiences and focus your messages to:
   - Interact with individual parents or community members.
   - Engage school staff with brief, timely updates.
   - Create a network with a larger group of education leaders.
   - Expand your staff development horizons.
   - Connect with media.

3. You can create new ties with your stakeholders and:
   - Build trust by being transparent with your community.
   - Alert the community of breaking news.

◆ Send community members to your website or blog for more information.

And, very importantly, Twitter is free! Once you get the hang of it, it's easy, quick, and fun. People like to use it—which means they are more likely to read your messages.

Tweets or Emails?

Although email is best for thoughtful, well-written messages, Twitter can provide connection with a large group of people immediately. And because Twitter is mobile and requires such brevity, it may be the tool of choice for many in your audience.

Using both email and Twitter strategically provides you with a way to target your communication. Sending too many emails will lead your audience to tune you out by either unsubscribing or deleting. Maintaining a consistent connection with your community is important, however, and Twitter provides an outlet for short, meaningful messages that keep your classroom, school, or district on the minds of your stakeholders.

Intersecting With a Wide Audience

People value interaction and become more trusting through regular, positive exchanges with their school and district leaders. Twitter can help you reach a portion of the community that you might not otherwise contact. Many people in the community look for easy ways to learn about what is going on in their neighborhood and at their school. They may (or may not) attend your once-a-year open house. It's not necessarily that they're not interested; it's just that they feel that the headlines are enough. They value their school, but they may only attend a meeting if they're dissatisfied with the way things are going. This silent majority—sometimes dubbed as "outsiders" or "nonparticipants"—can sometimes be turned into active supporters by following a school leader on Twitter. These folks want to know what's going on, to be included, and to be recognized even if they aren't active members of an advisory council, booster club, or committee. Creating a Twitter bridge to this silent majority may even inspire some to come to your open house the following year.

Shaping Your Story in Other Media

Reporters, editors, and bloggers follow Twitter and other social media to keep current and to mine for story ideas. Twitter can call attention to your story in a way that a formal press release does not. Superintendent Britten of Godfrey-Lee Public Schools—the administrator who at first didn't use Twitter and now tweets every day—learned this lesson after he posted a blog about his school's technology initiatives. At first, the blog didn't get much attention, but after a fellow superintendent read his blog, she tweeted: "Godfrey-Lee inspiring educators by not banning iPhones—Great forward thinking and leadership." Within eight hours, the Godfrey-Lee technology story hit the *Grand Rapids Press*.

Bad Tweets and Better Tweets

This may sound silly, but there's an art to Twitter. Creating a useful message of 140 characters, spaces included, takes practice. Twitter success requires being succinct and being personal—all in real time, while events are unfolding. Writing short is harder than writing long. We are reminded of the story of the author who submitted a 10,000-word manuscript to his publisher and told his editor, "Give me another month, and I can make it 5,000 words."

The quality of your Tweets is closely tied to your long-term success on Twitter. The bottom line is this: the more specific your Tweet is and the more tailored it is to a particular audience, the more compelling it will be. Let your voice come through by writing like you talk. This may take time and effort at first (free writing is a good tool for practice) but it pays dividends in building richer relationships with your followers. Draw in your audience by crafting the message to showcase its impact on the reader. When space allows, add detail—even one adjective. Also, be sure not to argue in your Tweets. This is a mistake many people make.

In addition, whenever you can, include a link to your web page, a related story, or a valued resource. As we mentioned earlier, shorten your URL using the Google URL Shortener (http://goo.gl). Go to the website and enter your URL. Click on Shorten and voila! You now have a shortened version that will better fit in your Tweet message.

Table 6.1 shows some examples of bad Tweets and better Tweets.

Table 6.1: Examples of Bad and Better Tweets

Tweet Categories	Bad Tweet	Better Tweet
School News Recom- mendations	Come to parent meeting on Tuesday.	Parents: Learn to spot signs your child is suffering from online bullying. Join roundtable discussion on Tuesday. *[link]*
	Support the flower sale.	Proceeds from flower sale to go to new library computers. *[link]*
	Book committee meets on Monday.	Book committee votes on new math text this Monday. *[link]*
	Reading an article on literacy.	Great article in LA Times *[link]* discusses implications of reading to children at home.
	See this article on gift giving.	The most beautiful gift in the world. *[link]*
	An insightful article on how parents teach children patience.	To teach children patience, a parent needs to breathe. *[link]*

Question	What is your opinion of student homework?	What is the ideal amount of time for sixth-grade homework? *[link]*
	What do you think about the online report cards?	Agree or disagree: online report cards are a good way to keep track of progress. *[link]*
	What did you think of our spring concert?	What was your favorite part of the spring concert? *[link]*
Response	@*[username]* Why would you say that?	@*[username]* Safety comes first. *[link]*
	@*[username]* I disagree.	@*[username]* Let's talk. Give me a call. *[link]*
	@*[username]* Thanks for the picture.	@*[username]* Great picture of your classroom. *[link]*
Slice of life	Tuna sandwich for lunch.	Lunch in caf. w/ Molly, a second grader. Tuna sandwiches for us both. *[link]*
	Winter is here.	First mitten sighting: children fil-ing off bus 38 this AM. *[link]*
	Celebrating 20 years of wedded bliss with my lovely wife this evening.	*(There is no better Tweet—this is not appropriate information to share.)*

Source: "Twitter: Not Just About Ham Sandwiches", by Kitty Porterfield & Meg Carnes, 2011, *Educational Leadership* 68(8) Online. ©2011 by ASCD. Reprinted with permission. Learn more about ASCD at www.ascd.org

Ten Twitter Dos and Don'ts

Following are ten Twitter dos and don'ts adapted from a list com-piled for lawyers who use Twitter (Pinnington, 2011):

1. **Don't take it too seriously.** Tweet to have some fun. Be careful, but remember that you are building relationships.

2. **Do consider the quality, not the quantity of your followers.** Work to make your followers those who care about education in your community.

3. **Do put your name on your Tweets.** If you aren't willing to put your name on something, it's probably not worth tweeting.

4. **Do write a clear description of yourself in your Twitter bio.** Help people know who they are following.

5. **Do tweet publicly and make it easy to follow your Tweets.** Tweets are meant to be public.

6. **Do be nice.** What goes around comes around.

7. **Don't post anything you wouldn't want your boss to read in the *New York Times*.** This recommendation seems so self-evident, yet people seem to forget it.

8. **Do inject some personal information, but not too much.** You need to share some personal information to better connect with your followers.

9. **Do share ideas, news, links, or other information that your followers will find interesting.** Send information that is practical, helpful, or interesting.

10. **Don't over-tweet. Tweets should be weighed, not counted.** Quality is far more important than quantity.

Educators Who Tweet

Not ready to start tweeting yet? It's okay to sign up and just listen to the conversation for a while. Here are some educators we follow and samples of their Tweets.

- @pammoran
  - **Bio:** Educator in Virginia, creating 21st century community learning spaces for all kinds of learners, both adults and young people.
  - **Sample Tweet:** This process is as relevant to observing in learning spaces as it is to capturing images with your camera http://t.co/BlpXbqhF
- @colonelb

- **Bio:** Husband, father, K–12 superintendent, retired Army officer, ultra distance runner & Red Wing fan. I wake up each morning looking to learn something new.
- **Sample Tweet:** Structural issues hurt U.S. math education; teacher training, support lag behind other countries http://bit.ly/hMOicw (via @earlyeditionapp)

- @DanielLFrazier

  - **Bio:** Superintendent, Sioux Central CSD, a 1:1 laptop school grades 4–12. Striving to transform education through technology integrated into instruction.
  - **Sample Tweet:** Are you an evangelist for 21st century learning? We need you. Blog post: http://t.co/epmGJKnK

- @johncarver

  - **Bio:** Supt. of Schools with 1:1 laptops in grades 6–12 and Virtual Reality capacity, committed to educational transformation
  - **Sample Tweet:** RT @ShellTerrell Meeting Challenges in the EFL Classroom/Pt 2:Using technology (by Christina Markoulaki) http://bit.ly/fxiIEi via @barbsaka

- @SuperScot

  - **Bio:** Superintendent of Saline Area Schools and Google Certified Teacher
  - **Sample Tweet:** Anyone have a good example of a data wall? Particularly at the elementary level.

- @ericconti

  - **Bio:** Burlington Public Schools Superintendent
  - **Sample Tweet:** Burlington school leaders confront bullying head-on—http://b.globe.com/fbVRc9 (via @BostonUpdate) #masschat #mvsachat #cpchat

Next Steps

1. Find three messages you have recently sent to your school community. Translate each of these messages into a Tweet.

How could you use them as a complement to your original communication?

2. Go to the Twitter.com home page. In the search box, type the name of your school division. What do the search results show?

Key Points

At its core, Twitter provides a way to listen to your community, be responsive, provide interesting content for people to share, and send your school's or district's message to a wider audience. Focusing on simple goals will help you develop a Twitter following and make it possible for you to sustain your effort.

Go to Twitter.com and get yourself an account today. Jump in!

CHAPTER

7 Blogging 101

I t's easy to create a blog site, but it's difficult to sustain one that develops a devoted and engaged audience. A blog entry brings with it different expectations than its distant print cousin, the "Superintendent's Corner" in the district newsletter. Blog readers expect a more conversational, less formal tone and will often want to interact and give feedback. Before you begin it is essential to identify your blogging goal and figure out what niche suits your personal style of leadership. Here are three possible goals:

1. Connect the community to the school.
2. Reveal the human side.
3. Provide "thought leadership."

Connecting the Community to the School

Jesse Kraft, who identifies himself as the lucky principal of Providence Elementary School in Fairfax, Virginia, publishes a weekly blog for parents and community members (http://providenceschool .wordpress.com). Written in an informal style and usually posted on Friday, Kraft's headlines underscore the emotional appeal of his content. Posts—including "Love Letter to the PTA" (2011c), "Hello, Young Man!" (2011a), and "We Miss You!" (2011b)—focus on a single happening from the school week and offer his take on the event.

Using WordPress, a popular blogging software program, Kraft also posts guidelines for comments on his blog that include protection of privacy and his expectation for appropriate, G-rated written expression. He also notes that topics for personal discussion are to be addressed with a phone call or email, not on the blog.

Patrick Larkin, a high school principal in Burlington, Vermont, keeps his community connected to school activities with frequent posts (http://burlingtonhigh.blogspot.com). Using Blogger (another blogging software program), Principal Larkin shines the light on school activities and groups, like Model United Nations or National Honor Society, frequently offering congratulations. He includes calendar updates and personal reflections on goals for student learning. One of the things you'll notice when visiting his blog is that he does not limit his blog to text.

Revealing the Human Side

A blog can provide a platform for a school leader who wants to establish a more personal connection with the community at large. People look for a human connection to their leaders; when done carefully, blogs can provide this connection. A good example of this is Principal Reflections (http://billcarozza.com), a blog written by Bill Carozza, a New Hampshire elementary principal. As the title implies, this blog shows the reader the thoughtful process behind educational decision making. In a post titled "Converted to Online Learning," Carozza tells the story of his experience with online teaching (Carozza, 2011). He peppers the story with personal details and reflections.

Superintendent Jerome Stewart from Midlothian Independent School District in Midlothian, Texas, often blogs about the people and events in his school district, frequently adding pictures and comments (http://drjstewart.wordpress.com). In one entry, "I am

Thankful to Be a Teacher" (Stewart, 2011), he tells a story of an important moment in his life that happened while he was watching a high school wrestling match:

> Recently, I was at a Midlothian High School home wrestling match. I did not have to attend the match; I wanted to be there. It was a choice. I wanted to see our kids wrestle.
>
> While watching the event, I did not notice a telephone call that came in on my cell phone clipped to my belt.

When the match was over, Stewart went back to his office, checked his phone, and saw that he had a message. His son, an Army Ranger serving a third tour of duty in Afghanistan, had called to tell his father that he had been wounded. Stewart lamented, "I missed my son's call."

However, rather than making this the story of his regret, Stewart immediately turned the story to connect this loss to teachers and the family time they give up for their students. His spare writing—short sentences and short paragraphs—and his matter-of-fact tone give the reader insight without sentimentality: "I can tell you, teachers cry. . . . I can tell you, teachers love. . . . I can tell you, I am thankful to be a teacher" (Stewart, 2011).

If you're going to publish a personal blog, write it yourself. To have it written in someone else's voice destroys the purpose of the blog and undermines your credibility. If you want a school division blog, and you don't like to write or don't have time to do it, ask someone else to do it under his or her own name and position. A blog by definition needs to be conversational and written in the voice of the blogger. The traditional "Superintendent's Corner" from the print newsletter, normally a more formal essay, does not translate successfully to the modern, informal blog.

Providing "Thought Leadership"

Pam Moran, the superintendent of Albemarle County Virginia Public Schools, hosts the blog A Space for Learning (http://spacesforlearning.wordpress.com), where she provides insights into topics all across the landscape of educational issues. She tackles federal and state educational policies and tells the stories behind issues happening in her school division.

The first lines of her blogs always offer a human connection, such as, "This week, I write for Savannah. She entered kindergarten, a tough little girl with stringy blond hair, pushing hard to create a space for herself" (Moran, 2011b).

She opened a Presidents' Day post (Moran, 2011a) as follows:

> Let us think of education as the means of developing our greatest abilities, because in each of us there is a private hope and dream which, fulfilled, can be translated into benefit for everyone and greater strength for our nation.

She followed with a list of eighteen quotes about education from presidents who exemplify the enduring commitment the United States has to children and learning.

Another educator whose blog provides thought leadership is Chris Lehmann, the founding principal of the Science Leadership Academy in Philadelphia, who authors Practical Theory (http://practicaltheory.org). Lehmann advocates for education ("Save the National Writing Project" [2010c]), passionately describes the value of high school sports ("An Important Win" [2010b]), and champions the contribution of technology to education ("Technology and the Whole Child" [2010a]).

Four other examples of school leaders who provide thought leadership via the blogosphere include:

1. George Wood, a high school principal in Stewart, Ohio, who serves as executive director of the Forum for Education and Democracy (http://forumforeducation.org/blogs/george-wood).

2. Charles Maranzano, a Hopatcong, New Jersey, superintendent, who writes about federal and state issues affecting education on Educational Leadership in Public Education (http://charlesmaranzano.blogspot.com).

3. Michael Smith, a superintendent in Oakland, Illinois, who posts on the Principals Page, where he often provides humorous insights into the life of a school administrator (www.principalspage.com/theblog).

4. David Britten, a retired U.S. Army officer who is now superintendent of Godfrey-Lee Public Schools in Michigan. He writes Colonel B's Corner (http://colonelb.posterous.com), where the reader will find postings with such titles as "A Rising or Setting Sun on K–12 Education?" (Britten, 2011b) and "The End of Common Sense in Lansing?" (Britten, 2011a).

In each of these examples, the leaders have a plan. They know what they're trying to achieve and what tone they will establish with their audience. Anyone wishing to create and sustain a blog over time must consider purpose and tone. Remember, like all social media endeavors, a blog is not a sprint. It's a marathon. Keep at it and engage your audience, and you can see great results.

Next Steps

1. What purpose could a blog serve for you? Who would read it, and how are they going to know you have one? What do you want them to do once they've read it?

2. Which of the previously listed categories fit your writing style best? Are there other categories that might also match your personal style?

Key Points

A blog is an opportunity for the superintendent or principal to cultivate a more personal relationship with his or her stakeholders and explore issues often overlooked in the daily hustle and bustle of school life. It is best to have a plan before you begin. Sustainability is a major issue.

8 Crafting Social Media Guidelines

When we asked our general counsel, who was also once a school board member, about the potential legal hazards for schools using social media, he said, "You've got to get with the program! If that's where parents and citizens are getting their news about education, then you've got to be there, too." We realize that not all lawyers serving school systems feel this way. Some superintendents and principals have pointedly told us that they have been forbidden by their legal departments from using social media platforms.

In debates about using social media in schools, worries about student safety, adult appropriateness, and fears of viral attacks against the district often overwhelm thoughtful discussion. Of course, every school leader should be concerned about these potential situations. Both the web and social media can be conduits for ill; however, the irony is that they also can be the very tools needed to help combat and overcome bad behavior. When someone is putting out false or harmful information about your school or district, you can use social media to reframe the conversation.

What Are We Afraid Of?

What makes social media seem so fearsome? Why does it seem different? For one thing, it's definitely *faster*. Social media can send messages across the world in hours—sometimes minutes. The reporting of the killing of Osama bin Laden illustrates how fast news travels these days. The first calls and questions from the *New York Times* reporters began a little before 10 p.m. when the White House posted an announcement that the President would soon make a statement. By 10:40 p.m., the *New York Times* had posted a one-line news alert of the death, already confirmed by two trusted sources (Brisbane, 2011). In forty minutes, the news had spread around the world.

On a more personal level, most of us have pushed the Send button on an email addressed to the wrong person. The message is already in the wrong inbox by the time we realize our mistake. It is an occupational hazard of our time in which communication can be delivered instantaneously.

Messages can also travel *farther* with social media. A video of a confrontation between a school security guard and a student, surreptitiously filmed and posted on YouTube, can bring indignation from across the country. More than one superintendent (or CEO or elected official) has felt the sting of a rumor run wild in cyberspace.

In addition, there is no guarantee that the messages that travel on social media wings (often presented as "news" or "fact") have been vetted in even a cursory way. As much as schools decry the reporting accuracy of their local television stations and newspapers, the fact is that there is an organization behind newspaper and television stories, and they usually represent at least a modicum of truth telling. With social media in the community, *no one* is responsible for checking the accuracy of a message.

Additionally, social media messages written in cyberspace become part of a permanent record. On most social media platforms, it is hard to erase completely what someone has said—or what has been said about someone. Offhand comments, badly crafted humor, and misdirected criticism can all have unpleasant consequences. We all have to be careful.

Balancing Risks Versus Benefits

As always, school leaders must balance the risks and benefits. Remember, we pay our legal counsel to think of the worst-case scenarios and then offer suggestions to prevent them. What might at first feel like an unequivocal "no" might, on further reflection, contain dependent clauses. After all, do schools ban all physical education because a student might sprain an ankle running around the track? Given the potential legal issues, however, all districts must craft social media policies and practices that work for their own community within their own state laws. There is no one-size-fits-all communication policy any more than there is a one-size-fits-all instruction guide for all students.

Media policies should be about adults communicating with other adults—staff members, parents, and community members. We must be able to distinguish between how we communicate with adults and how we communicate with our students. We should be sophisticated enough to craft policies and practices that cover both kinds of conversations. After all, the worksheets we hand out to first graders do not (and should not) look like the newsletters (or blogs) we write for their parents.

An Ounce of Prevention

Let's go back to that sprained ankle we mentioned. What do schools do to prevent injuries in gym class? They provide students with trained teachers to supervise them. They enforce safety rules and ensure that equipment is in good working order. Teachers teach students the correct technique for use in sports activities and encourage healthy training to build strength. (After all, students don't run a mile the first day out!)

Schools and districts can safely learn to build their social media capabilities by doing the following:

- **Crafting straightforward social media policies that are easy to understand and use, and then putting them in place.** We describe such policies later in the chapter and offer specific strategies for writing such guidelines.

- **Providing staff development for faculty and staff.** A survey by the National Cyber Security Alliance, a nonprofit group that works with the U.S. Department of Homeland Security to promote computer security awareness, reports that, although a majority of teachers (55 percent) "strongly agrees" that online safety should be covered in the curriculum, over a third of teachers (36 percent) had themselves received no training by their school districts during the previous year, and another 40 percent had received only one to three hours of training (Marklein, 2011). This training can include many topics, such as how to manage a class in which students do online research, how to teach students to protect themselves online, and how to use helpful software and security aids.

- **Learning how to react if there is a problem.** Leaders proficient in social media use are quite clear that the way to deal with rumor and distortion on the web or in social media platforms is to overwhelm it with truth. For example, if someone attacks your district on Facebook, keep putting out the good news, and you will drown out those who seek to sully your good name. Chances are your supporters (if you've been diligent about building strong relationships) will cover the attack with praise and affirmation.

Like the track coach, then, we must build a safety net of training and practice. Will our kids (and our staff members) sometimes stub their toes anyway? You bet. But that's what learning is all about.

Ultimately, our counsel's advice to us was that leaders are no less responsible for the quality of what they put out in social media than they are in quality of their newsletters. It doesn't matter what the media is. The responsibility is the same.

Friday Faux Pas

The Mayo Clinic Center for Social Media (http://socialmedia.mayoclinic.org) posts a column titled *Friday Faux Pas* that highlights missteps in social media made by health-related organizations. The Center believes that social media is overwhelmingly a force for good, but that potential problems inevitably occur. The series looks at each faux pas, highlights how it might have been prevented, and notes how the organization responded (Schwarz, 2011).

Next Steps

1. Using examples of other social media policies, draft one for your school or district.

2. What do people need to know? Create an outline for staff training in the use of social media in your school or district.

Where to Start

Many districts that have implemented social media practices have yet to establish guidelines. At one meeting of thirty school public relations professionals, we found that they were all "in the process" of writing guidelines—even though they were already engaged in using social media.

School districts create social media guidelines to define social media use and provide a framework and safeguards for success. These guidelines facilitate the implementation of social media strategies, give participants the information they need to collaborate effectively, and make it possible to respond quickly in emergencies.

Start by reviewing the guidelines crafted by others. Check out the Policy Database at Social Media Governance (http://socialmediagovernance.com/policies.php; Boudreaux, 2011) to review social media policies from corporations, nonprofits, local governments, and universities. For example, you can review the Coca-Cola Company's three-page summary of its online social media principles that describe the company's core values as they are to be implemented in the online community.

The Policy Database also has a three-page summary from Ball State University that offers definitions and policies for all social media sites, including personal sites. It also outlines the expectation that all federal requirements, such as the Family Education Rights and Privacy Act (FERPA), will be followed (Boudreaux, 2011). School districts interpret FERPA laws differently, so check with your legal counsel regarding policy guidelines unique to your school.

Some organizations create separate policies unique to a specific social media venue. For example, on the Policy Database, you'll find specific blog policies (see, for example, FedEx and General Motors) and comment policies (see, for example, Iowa Hospital Association) (Boudreaux, 2011). There's a lot of information available to help school leaders get a sense of the big picture when crafting guidelines.

Another excellent resource for developing school social media guidelines is a post on My Island View, a blog written by Tom Whitby (http://tomwhitby.wordpress.com). The post is titled "World's Simplest Online Safety Policy" (Whitby, 2011). Although the post focuses mostly on guidelines for the student use of social media in classroom learning environments, it also addresses the three main federal acts governing school information—FERPA, Children's Internet Protection Act (CIPA), and Children's Online Privacy Protection Act (COPPA). Whitby also provides insights important to leaders who want to open social media channels to interact with their adult community. In advocating for the greater use of technology, he provides clear guidance.

Another source of guidelines and policies comes from web expert Jill Kurtz (2009), who advises creating a social media policy that's complementary to your school culture. She suggests these considerations:

- Make a status assessment of your communication plan. Involve all areas of the organization. Identify the ways you communicate (good and bad) throughout the organization.
- Stay open to opportunities. Social media offers new options. Be open to how it can help you engage with your community, collaborate, solve problems, provide customer services, increase efficiency, and more.
- Make sure your policy is flexible enough to adapt as the world around you evolves.
- Take acceptable risks. Risks lead to innovation and growth. But be sure you cover legal liabilities and are compliant with the law.

Some of your staff members who will be representing the school will be new to using social media. Having guidelines is especially helpful for them. But guidelines are just that—they're guidelines. The need to be professional in the digital realm is rooted in common sense. It is key to appoint someone in your district to oversee those who are posting on your social media channels. This individual who monitors and provides feedback to your digital writers also serves as a reminder to writers that the goal of all district posting is to support the school's mission.

Guidelines for Your Community

As you launch a new platform, a Facebook page for example, let the community know how they can contribute; create specific guidelines for them as well. For example, here's part of the policy from Union County North Carolina's Public Schools Facebook page:

> All posting of comments on this page are at the discretion of the page administrators. The intent of this policy is not to keep any negative or critical information from being posted, but to protect the privacy and rights of UCPS staff and

students. Naming specific employees or students in a negative way will not be allowed. The page administrators will review all postings to make sure they do not run afoul of the rules nor of the district's Acceptable Use Guidelines regarding Internet access and practices. (Union County Public Schools, n.d.)

The Facebook policy of Kansas City, Missouri's Park Hill School District encourages interaction from users but is clear that they are not responsible for comments or wall postings made by visitors to the page. Part of their policy says:

Comments posted also do not in any way reflect the opinions or positions of the school district. Park Hill asks that people making comments on the page show respect for their fellow users by ensuring the discussion remains civil, especially since Facebook allows children as young as 13 to join. Comments are also subject to Facebook's Terms of Use and Code of Conduct. Remember that your name and photo will be seen next to your comment, visible to the hundreds of visitors to the page. We reserve the right, but assume no obligation, to remove comments that are racist, sexist, abusive, profane, violent, obscene, spam, contain falsehoods or are wildly off-topic, or that libel, incite, threaten or make ad hominem attacks on students, employees, guests or other individuals. (Park Hill School District, n.d.)

Explain your expectations to your community members by posting guidelines on every social media channel you open. Will they be able to comment? If they comment, how soon can they expect a response? Should they expect a response? If you're not going to allow comments, explain why. Update your guidelines as issues arise.

Guidelines for Critical Moments

Being prepared in an emergency—for a digital attack—should be part of your guidelines. For example, what will you do if you must face an assault by a parent Facebook group that is posting untrue information about a school incident? Establishing guidelines now for how you will handle negative comments helps you to implement quickly the steps you need to take in this kind of crisis. Your guidelines should address such topics as transparency, dialogue, and the social media platforms you'll use. A team should be designated to provide a rapid response, which may include talking to the person responsible for the posting, addressing the rumors, and correcting them through your own platforms. It might also include participating on the offending page by posting the correct information.

Next Steps

1. Find two or three school pages on Facebook that include the schools' Facebook policies. Make a list of the items they address. What are the commonalities?

2. What would you consider when putting together a steering committee to develop a social media policy for your school? Who would you include?

Key Points

Using social media well means that we must be sure to have strong policies in place, train our staff members in good-use strategies, and be prepared to say, "We made a mistake." And when mistakes happen, we can also use social media to overcome the effects of an error.

Social media policies are readily available on the web. Reviewing the policies of others is a good way to begin to develop your own policy, both for your staff and your community. Customizing your guidelines and continuing to update them regularly will keep you on track.

9 What We Say and How We Say It Matter

If we could always work face to face, leadership would be much easier. However, the size of our institutions and the breadth of our jobs usually limit the number of face-to-face exchanges that can happen in a day. Fortunately, new technologies allow us to reach more people in ways that are still perceived as helpful and even personal. Tools like Facebook and Twitter can do the work for us.

We've already established that the old ways of sending messages home from school don't work well anymore. So we work hard to get the word out to our audiences in new ways, only to have people say, "Gosh, we didn't know" or "No one told us that." Even if we are using new tools, we can still miss the mark.

Roadblocks

There are many impediments to getting our messages through. Among them are the following:

- **Stakeholder overload**—Every day there are thousands of new messages competing for our attention. It is simply impossible for any adult (let alone a parent) to pay attention to everything stamped "Important!" Inevitably, things will be missed. (Think about how you navigate your own mailbox, email, and voicemail.) In frustration and exhaustion, people simply stop reading or listening.

- **The delete key**—Your stakeholders don't recognize that your message is important to them. It just looks like all the other junk mail that arrives on their screen, so it is never opened. (In fact, some organizations have given up using HTML to make their e-blasts look professional and have reverted instead to sending important messages in plain text because surveys show that readers tend to think that plain text messages are more apt to be personal!)

- **Message irrelevance**—Sometimes, despite what *we* think, the messages we send simply aren't important to our stakeholders. Sometimes, our clients are actually making good decisions for themselves when they ignore what we are saying!

Given these (and other) challenges, our job is to make our messages stand out. This is not easy—even though we are talking to parents about their children. It means we have to look not only at our communication tools, but also at *what* we are saying.

Making Things Sticky

Fascinating research about how our brains work and how people make decisions is underway. In *The Tipping Point*, Malcolm Gladwell (2000) introduced the concept of the "sticky idea"—an idea that catches on, that causes people to take notice or, better yet, to change their behavior.

At the same time, two brothers in California—Chip Heath, a professor of organizational behavior at Stanford University, and Dan Heath, a consultant at Duke Corporate Education and former researcher at Harvard Business School—were asking why some stories are told over and over and become urban legends, whereas other good stories never get traction.

They began watching ideas more carefully and asking themselves questions like, "How can we nurture our ideas so that they succeed in the world?" and "What is the difference between the message that we remember and the ones we forget?" (Heath & Heath, 2007).

According to the Heath brothers, there are six principles that, used in combination, will give your idea *stickiness*, that quality that causes your idea to be "understood and remembered, and have a lasting impact" and that will "change your audiences' opinions or behavior" (Heath & Heath, p. 8). We call this the "head and heart test," recalling Jonah Lehrer's admonition to reach out to both sides of the brain. The six principles are as follows.

1. **Simple:** According to Heath and Heath, "The more we reduce the amount of information in an idea, the stickier it will be" (2007, p. 46). With so many theories of effective teaching and learning and such heavy pressure on parents to raise perfect children, parents look to teachers and school leaders to help them make the best decisions they can about their children's education. Perhaps one of the best ways school leaders can help parents is to sort through the conflicting messages about parenting and education and say simply, "These are the most important ideas and issues. Focus your attention here."

   The Heaths (2007) also cite psychologists who have found that people are driven to make bad decisions by too much complexity. Uncertainty can paralyze us. Simple messages help people avoid paralysis, or bad decisions, by reminding them what is important. Simple, short messages can be easily reinforced using social media.

2. **Unexpected:** The first challenge in sending any message is getting people's attention and keeping it. As Heath and Heath (2007) note, "Unexpected ideas are more likely to stick because surprise makes us pay attention and think" (p. 68). Add a little mystery to the equation, and people will be hooked. How about the superintendent mentioned previously who made Facebook a teaching tool instead of banning it on school computers? The message conveyed by his action—that he was willing to take some risks in order to reach his stakeholders—was a surprise.

3. **Concrete:** Beginning learners crave concreteness. The best teachers know this intuitively—they start with a story or an object and build from there. Young Montessori schoolchildren learn math with beads and rods that they can touch, move, and measure. Adult learners need this as well. Concrete language helps adults learn new concepts, especially abstract concepts. Why else would Aesop have written his advice in fables? Why do business schools teach using a case study? When you welcome a new class of seventh graders to the middle school, you take them on a tour of the building and show them something real.

4. **Credible:** We tend to believe ideas, the Heaths say, if we have the recommendation of people we trust or if we can relate them to things we already know. It is also easier to believe a new idea if it is rich with details or backed up with some clear statistics to provide context (Heath & Heath, 2007). That doesn't mean your budget presentation needs to be 125 frames long, but it might mean you include endorsements for your plan from important community leaders.

5. **Emotional:** According to the Heaths, "For people to take action, they have to *care*" (Heath & Heath, 2007, p. 168). Can you define the purpose of your organization or your latest initiative in a way that would motivate people to *care* about it? Can you—in 140 characters or fewer—justify why you are asking volunteers to donate their time, taxpayers to contribute their money, and parents to trust you with their children? Can your messages generate that much emotional energy?

6. **Tell stories:** The Heaths have found that "the right stories make people act" (Heath & Heath, 2007, p. 206). Stories are simple and concrete, and they usually contain some emotional content and surprise. Good stories are full of wisdom and invite the listener to take a journey or embark on a meaningful adventure. Stories can show how an existing problem might be reframed and offer alternative solutions. Stories can shed light on human relationships and communication. Stories can set an example. The best stories can *be* your message. Do you want to introduce a new instructional practice? Instead of touting a list of why this way is better, describe what you saw when you visited a

classroom where the teachers and students were engaged in this new learning technique.

Getting Straight to the Point

Over and over again, parents have told us that they need to know:

- Where they need to be and when (to pick up their children from play practice, for instance)
- How many cupcakes to bring
- Where and how they can meet their child's teachers
- How to get timely information on their child's progress

Can you find ways to send information that your stakeholders want to know—using both old and new technologies—in messages that are simple, concrete, credible, unexpected, and wrapped in a story with some emotional punch? Can you build trust with your stakeholders by taking time to have these simple conversations? For example:

- **Tweet**—"High notes and low notes! Holiday concert, Friday, 7pm."
- **Facebook**—"Kudos to all the parents who supported our yard sale. We raised over $2000 for new band instruments." Or, "Couldn't have done it without you! Funds will upgrade student computers immediately!"
- **Website home page**—"Congratulations to Superintendent Jane Meister [*pictured with eleventh-grade science students*] who has been named state superintendent of the year. _More_."

Next Steps

1. Take three messages you sent out during the previous week. Do they pass the stickiness test? How could you change them to make them stickier?

2. Go back to the issue you identified in chapter 3 (page 39)—the single issue that needs more communication. Create two sticky messages you can use in this situation.

The Language of Social Media

Our former English teachers, including the awesome Mr. Ferber, taught us well. Every sentence had a noun, a verb, and a few carefully chosen modifiers. Run-on sentences were broken into separate, discrete thoughts. Sentence fragments were forbidden. All paragraphs contained an introductory sentence, a concluding sentence, and a number of sentences in the middle that expanded or supported the thesis. Random ideas were edited out and put in paragraphs of their own.

There was no room for a one-sentence paragraph.

According to Mr. Ferber, proper punctuation and spelling were next to godliness. Exclamation marks were rarely called for. An A paper could become a C paper based on poor punctuation alone. Messages like "U R Gr8!" or "Thnx!" did not compute. Indeed, the language of social media has its own rules and guidelines.

Write Short

Poets and headline writers have a head start on the rest of us. Their job—and now ours—is saying a *lot* in very few words. It takes time and thought to create an exciting invitation in a 140-character Tweet. "Come to the holiday party" might be better written as, "Chocolate cookies, sparkling punch and holiday music. Thurs, 12/14, 7pm. Clover ES. Come! Bring family, friends."

Writing short is important on the web too. Think about how you read a news article. The headline catches your eye. You read the first paragraph, maybe two. You head for the last paragraph. Then, if you are interested, you may read the stuff in between.

That is how people read what you write on the web (or don't read it, if they can't easily get the information they want). So, for an important story, the headline goes on your website home page, followed by a two-sentence introduction of the topic and explanation of why it's important to your readers. For example:

Principal Named to State Panel
Pembrook High School Principal, James Eikenberry, was named by Governor Elson to his new state curriculum review board. The board will make recommendations for major changes in K–12 instruction which will affect our schools. *More*

On the "More" page, you can place links to the Governor's press release, the story in the local paper, and/or a statement by the principal or James' superintendent, such as "We are so proud that Jim has been named . . ." Folks who want the detail will click through.

Writing short is the rule for blogs too. Each post should be one page, double spaced—three hundred words maximum. More than that produces "blog bog down." Focus on one idea—think of the blog as an extended paragraph rather than a shortened essay. Quick sentences, maybe even ones without a verb? (Sorry, Mr. Ferber—we are breaking your time-honored rules again.) Use punchy vocabulary: "a tangled web" rather than "an issue." Present your idea clearly, but also take time to catch your readers' attention with some energy. Lengthy, tired blogs are passed over, just like tired superintendents' messages in the district newsletter were.

Write Like You Speak

Because these days we depend so much on the written word, our blogs and our Tweets need to sound like us. We need to add character to the characters on the page. This also demands more *un*learning for many of us. As Mr. Ferber's English students, we learned that what we put on the page needed a formal voice, not our conversational self. Things have changed.

Being informal does *not* mean being sloppy. Because the published word stays around—especially in the virtual realms—and becomes part of our permanent record, we need to take care. We need to get the facts straight, be judicious with personal information, and be careful and sparing in our judgments.

At the same time, your stakeholders—your parents, staff members, and your community supporters—want to know who you are. They are hungry to understand their leader. Write as if you are in conversation with your stakeholders. Write as if you expect a response. (Indeed, if you are lucky, a response will come.) Write as if you want to know what your stakeholders are thinking. They may surprise you.

Remember, this new kind of writing takes practice; it might help to get yourself a trusted writing buddy who will read and edit your work. Here are some more writing rules that Mr. Ferber didn't teach.

Write to Connect

Understanding who your audience is—your staff, the young parents, the city council—and knowing what is of value to them is essential to making yourself heard. A school system that covers the front page of the website with vast amounts of data from statewide test results (we've seen it) has missed the point. Of course, people are interested in test scores, and they should be posted on the website— but not in endless detail on the home page. That space is reserved for headlines and time-sensitive information your parents and community particularly want to hear, such as "District test scores up. Third and fifth grades make gains in math. Fourth-grade reading scores improve. _More_."

The more you speak to your stakeholders' interests, the greater the bond you build between them, your school, and your district. You want people to develop the habit of looking to you and your website, Twitter feed, or Facebook page first for important news. Make yourself quotable.

Write With Passion

Even if you are writing about the budget, talk about your mission, about the kids who will learn, about the community that will be served. Get granular when you are talking about how the dollars will help in the classroom. Be as concrete about the benefits of what you are proposing as you can. Give people something to get excited about. Give them something to believe in. If you simply can't find the passion, then find someone else to write the story.

Focus on the Verbs

Verbs are the words in any sentence that pack the punch. In general, we all use far too many iterations of the verb *to be*, like *is* and *will be*. Seize a verb that moves! Avoid the passive tense altogether. Replace "The meeting was called to order by Aisha" with "Aisha led a vigorous discussion."

A corollary to this rule is to use adjectives and adverbs sparingly. They tend to weaken your sentence. Write "The audience was visibly moved by the children's performance," not "The play was full of very sad, tear-jerking moments."

Write to Figure Out What You Are Thinking

People often say to us, "I just can't get started. I don't know what to say." One of the closely kept secrets about good writing is that many of the best pieces start in a dense fog. You know that you have a message, but you can't quite define it. That's the time to sit at the keyboard and type whatever comes from your fingers. Don't edit—just keep typing.

The wisdom may come clear in the first few sentences, or it may take many paragraphs for you to get to the heart of the matter. If you don't begin to put words on the paper, however, you will never succeed in transitioning your ideas to the screen. They will just rattle around in your head, and eventually get lost in the rest of the day's business.

Start anywhere—in the middle, at the conclusion, or halfway in between. Put down one sentence, and then keep going. Before too long, a theme will emerge, and you'll exclaim, "That's what I meant!" Never wait until you have it all figured out. Just start writing.

Edit—A Lot

Although you can write anything, in any way, the first time through, you owe it to your readers to be rigorous in your editing and polishing processes. It's a good idea to get other people to review your work before you publish it (in print or on the web). Sometimes just a few small changes can make a big difference—and can save you from making a hugely embarrassing mistake.

Create a Structure

In the matter of structure, Mr. Ferber was not entirely wrong. He worried about paragraphs. We suggest that you look at the whole piece. Don't let your readers get lost trying to follow your train of thought. Sprinkle plenty of road signs around (like headers, carefully chosen conjunctions, and connecting sentences) so that at all times your readers will know exactly where they have been and where you are leading them.

Point to Additional Sources

In the old days, a term paper or an essay was not complete without a detailed reference section. Today's readers still like directions to information sources where they can explore subjects on their own, but now, they are mostly looking for web resources. Especially on the web, Facebook, and Twitter, the more direct links you can provide the better. Remember, write short, and then let the reader explore on his or her own.

Triage for Your Readers

The virtual world is already filled with junk—flashy advertisements, mind-numbing nonsense, and energy-sucking communication—that masquerades as relationship building. People need, and will respond to, messages that help them sort out what is important and where they should put their attention. Using a few well-shaped sentences or paragraphs creates a framework in which you, your parents, your staff, and your community can discuss the important issues.

Writing well is hard work. It takes time. But it clears the brain and leads to better conversations. So sharpen your (metaphorical) pencil and get to work.

Next Steps

1. Choose a message you would like to communicate. Write three different Tweets (no more than 140 characters) that tell the story in different ways.

2. Take a newsletter column or recent memo that you wrote. Edit it to say the same thing in half the words and with twice the passion!

Key Points

Our messages carry no weight if no one pays attention to them. We need to be heard above the thousands of voices on the airwaves every day. We need to make our messages sticky. They need to be simple, unexpected, concrete, credible, emotional, and they need to contain (or be contained in) stories. Sticky messages help to build relationships.

Writing for the web and social media is different from writing a dissertation—or even a column for the newsletter. You need to write short, make a connection with your reader, and include resources where your readers can get more information. Editing is essential—you can never be too short.

CHAPTER 10

Listening to Social Media

For better or worse, today we face fewer and fewer barriers in our efforts to shape public opinion. Consider the following:

- A Facebook message can be posted or a Tweet sent in an instant from anywhere: behind a desk, in the grocery store, or on the soccer field sidelines.

- Facebook friends can add their own testimonies, stories, pictures, and videos, and Tweets can be endlessly retweeted, expanding the audience further.

- Online petition sites, such as Care2 (www.Care2.com), offer petitions as a free service. Paper is no longer a necessity!

- People communicate online 24–7; the online meeting room is always open! Social media is the new party line.

- People can avoid personal risk online—they can remain anonymous, and many more people lurk on websites (that is, read but not participate directly in the conversation).

Social media may make you feel more vulnerable, but remember: it can also make you more powerful. The key to using it effectively and not allowing your school to be vulnerable is to sharpen your listening skills.

Sharpening Your Listening Skills

For years, we've understood that listening is a critical component of effective communication. Listening has an even more important role in social media. Listening online gives leaders insight into their communities in a way that face-to-face meetings and even surveys often do not. Comments on social media can expose the true feelings of stakeholders; they may say different things about you when they think you are not listening. It's not always pretty, so you have to develop a thick skin and a process to identify which comments are an accurate reflection of what your stakeholders really think. Here's how you might start your online listening.

Develop Goals: What Are You Trying to Accomplish?

The first step is to develop a listening strategy to guide you through the ever-changing world of conversations that others are having about you in the blogosphere. The listening process is ongoing and sharpens your awareness of what's being said outside school boundaries. The amount of listening you could do is limitless, so put some boundaries on it by establishing focused goals. This makes the process, and the time you devote to it, productive. Your initial goals may look like these:

- Develop awareness of the issues discussed in online conversations.
- Learn where your community goes online.
- Identify the influential online voices and sites.
- Analyze your district's or school's online reputation.

Specify Time: How Often Will You Listen?

Will you listen in once a day, twice a day, once a week? The amount of time you allocate needs to be in direct proportion to the goals you've set for listening. In the beginning, listening once or twice a week may be enough. Nevertheless, you need to be flexible;

if there's a controversy brewing, more frequent trips to your listening posts will serve you well. As you engage in more online media platforms yourself, your listening schedule will expand, but your reading and scanning efficiency will also increase. You should listen at least daily to your school district's social media platforms. If you have a school Facebook page that's very active with folks posting throughout the day, then you may need to check it two to three times a day.

Designate Personnel: Who Will Listen?

There's no one-size-fits-all approach to identifying your social media listener or listeners. This person or persons will typically summarize and distribute reports and act as the eyes and ears for the district. If your district has full-time staff devoted to marketing and communication, it makes sense to tap one of them for the job. Smaller districts can form a *listening team* comprised of staff members representing various areas of responsibility that will share the listening. Having a common collection tool and a schedule will organize your efforts.

Develop a Collection Tool: How Will You Record Your Observations?

A good collection system is one that efficiently aligns with the goals you've set for listening. It allows the person listening to scan for information and record meaningful data. Table 10.1 (page 106) is one example of a collection tool organized by keyword searches that aligns categories with the school's listening goals. The source, issue, and context categories identify where your online audience is, what they're talking about, and how the conversation characterizes your school. The listener will use the influence category to evaluate the credibility of the voice and the amount of weight that the voice might carry in the community. The listener can use the comments column to add details that may be useful in understanding the information. Once you have mapped the comments, you can

Table 10.1: Sample Social Media Collection Tool

Keyword: *Mountain Top Central Schools*				
Source	Issue or Topic	Influence (High, Medium, or Low)	Context (Negative, Positive, or Neutral)	Comments
Washpost.com	School uniforms	Low	Negative	National story; no local focus
Journal.com	School uniforms	High	Neutral	Local source; quotes local parents
Facebook	Kindergarten orientation	High	Negative	Lack of understanding about dates, times, and registration process
Mountain Top Mom Blog	Class size	High	Negative	Highly critical of school board decision to increase class size; contains misinformation
Twitter	Teacher appreciation week	Medium	Positive	Thirty-five retweets of superintendent's Tweet on teacher appreciation week

determine which ones need attention. (We'll talk about how to do that later in this chapter in the section on search engines.)

Creating a simple system and automating everything you can are essential to the success of the listening process.

Decide What to Do Next: How Will You Use What You've Heard?

Once you've done the listening and collecting, you need to learn to triage situations based on what you have uncovered. Here are some questions to ask:

- **How will you evaluate what you hear?** Figure out who and what have real influence. Watch for comments from key stakeholders in the community. What do they know that you don't?

- **Will you share your insights?** Develop a process for sharing what you learn with key staff and even with your community.

- **Will you respond?** You probably won't respond at first—unless you are dealing with malicious and inaccurate information. You should listen first, collect information, and consult with interested parties before you respond.

- **How will you respond?** Will you respond online? In a media release? With a letter to a particular person? Make the response match the situation. If someone has posted a question or comment on your district's Facebook page, for example, you must respond there to demonstrate to your entire Facebook audience that you're paying attention and anxious to interact.

Next Steps

1. Listening to your community and taking the time to learn about your constituents' needs are the best types of service you can offer. Think of a time when listening to your community helped you to solve a problem before it turned into a crisis.

2. Who would you recommend do the listening for your school or division? How much time will you allocate for listening? How will you analyze the results and share findings?

Search Engines Make Listening Easy

The first rule of communication success is to know your audience. In the old days, you might have invested time and money in a survey to learn your community's views. Yet paper-and-pencil surveys often failed to provide the inside view we needed because of the amount of time that elapsed between administering the survey and seeing the results. By the time a survey revealed the lack of support for a bond referendum, for example, the election was all but over.

Today, search engines—many of them free—allow you to listen and gather information in real time about your community's attitudes and beliefs around topics. These search engines scan existing blogs, newspaper stories, articles, and papers to find what has been written. The immediacy of the feedback provides you with an early warning system to keep you in the know.

One school leader shared with us how she found out the hard way about the need to listen to social media. Her story involved the inappropriate behavior of a school employee at a Thursday-evening event on school grounds. A cell phone camera captured the incident, and the video was uploaded to YouTube. It spread rapidly in cyberspace, but school leaders were unaware of it until Monday morning when they were alerted by a phone call from a reporter.

What stunned this principal, she said, was how fast the story spread and how little time they had to deal with it. Had they known earlier, they would have at least sent a message out to parents to get ahead of the story. As it was, they had to play catch-up and suffered from negative public opinion.

In an example from another district, a fan at a football game deliberately provoked a school security guard while a friend captured it on his cell phone camera. That video was also posted to YouTube, causing a nationwide debate about the roles and responsibilities of school guards (who are not police officers). The fallout kept the school's security office responding for days.

It's common for leaders today to be forced unexpectedly into the court of public opinion, and it's impossible to predict when it will happen or why. What might be a headline in one district is treated as a yawn somewhere else. Listening to what your community is saying (and watching) online gives schools and leaders a heads-up to potential problems. Search engines are a fast and efficient way to do this.

Creating a Listening Post

Setting up a "listening post" means creating an electronic process that brings the news to you. Free and simple tools are available for conducting *ego searches*—the popular name for monitoring blogs and news for mentions of your school, your superintendent, your topics, your issues, and so on. Conducting ego searches allows you to stay informed.

Start by selecting your online listening post, which is typically a *newsreader*, a type of software that collects and displays all the information from your keyword searches. Your reader updates automatically every time new information containing your keyword appears in the searched feeds. Many newsreaders are free, such as Google Reader (www.google.com/reader), which is one of the most popular. Simply go to the site and sign up.

Once you've signed up, you select your *feeds* (the sites that you want searched to collect news for you). Go to the feed, sign up, and enter your keywords. Consider starting small with just two well-established feeds. Here are some feeds that are worth a look:

- Technorati (http://technorati.com)
- Yahoo! News (http://news.yahoo.com)
- Addict-o-matic (http://addictomatic.com)
- Social Mention (www.socialmention.com)
- Ice Rocket (www.icerocket.com)

Currently, social networking sites such as Facebook, Twitter, and YouTube, do not have a feature you can use to have searches sent to your reader. If your community is on these sites—and as we've already established, they probably are—you will have to set up and monitor your own searches on those sites. It's worth your time and attention especially if you're dealing with a crisis situation. Go to each site and type in your school name in the search box.

Identifying Keywords

As we already mentioned, *keywords* are the words that you plug into search engines to collect what people are saying about you. Here is a short list of examples to get you started:

- Name of your school district
- Name of your superintendent
- Topics (standing items of interest, such as curriculum, athletics, report cards, and so on)
- Issues (items dictated by events, such as redistricting and bond vote)

Finding the right keywords to describe the items on your list is a process of refinement. Your search results will show you where you need to tighten up the language. For example, the keywords *Smith County bond vote* may be too broad. Changing your keywords to *Smith County Schools bond referendum* may be a simple way to refine the list and make the results more relevant.

Asking staff and parents for words they use to describe the issues you are following is one good way to pinpoint precise keywords. Google offers another free resource: the Google Keyword Tool Box (www.googlekeywordtool.com). Simply enter a few descriptive words or phrases, and a list of keywords appears on your screen. It's like a thesaurus for keywords.

Next Steps

1. Brainstorm a list of topics and issues that are important for your school division's listening post. Then edit your list to identify the precise keywords to identify for each.

2. Make a list of places online where your community goes to talk about issues and topics related to your school.

Key Points

Community conversations are being held on the web with or without school leaders' knowledge. Once these conversations start, word can travel fast. Schools and districts must become good listeners and use this information to learn what community members say when the filters are off. Be faithful to your goals and develop a willingness to evaluate your progress regularly. This will help you to make listening an integral component of your communication plan.

Setting up a listening post requires patience and trial and error. When you have created an efficient one, you'll only need a small block of time for daily (or weekly) reading. Your listening post is like an early warning system that you can use to decide the appropriate next steps.

11 Crisis Management and Social Media

In a crisis, school leadership skills all come together—or not. In crisis, social media can be an important tool for the leader.

Here is how the superintendent of the Nixa Public Schools in Nixa, Missouri, employed Twitter during a series of serious thunderstorms and a tornado watch:

6:22 a.m., May 8—"We've cleared out all our trailers' due to the bad weather. I promise we'll take good care of the kids during this scary time."

7:03 a.m., May 8—"No damage at any of our schools as of right now. Inman has lost power, but we are taking care of that."

7:28 a.m., May 8—"We do have some minor damage around the district. Nothing major that we can tell. Checking things out right now."

7:47 a.m., May 8—"We have a light pole down across the JH track. Minor damage at other places. Keeping students out of mobile classrooms for a while."

7:53 a.m., May 8—"We are now releasing the elementary students to complete their bus routes from the morning."

8:22 a.m., May 8—"Power back on at Inman
Elementary. We are in the all clear mode.
Students are able to go back out to mobile
classrooms."

8:36 a.m., May 8—"B/c of damage from the
storm, the NJH Walk for a Cause has been
canceled for Sat. Bring in canned goods on Mon
or Tues for Least of These."

Crisis management is simply common sense at the speed of light.
The issues that confront a school leader in a crisis are often similar
to the issues he or she faces on an average day—but they are issues
on steroids. In a crisis, the communication skills that are important
to a leader every day become more important by many orders of
magnitude.

In their book *The Politics of Crisis Management*, Boin, 't Hart,
Stern, and Sundelius (2008) make clear what many leaders know
intuitively: in a crisis, information is "a key currency of power" (p.
34). Leaders, they say, must ensure that the people they are leading
trust the information they are being told (Boin et al., 2008).

Timing Is Everything

In most crises, things happen fast, very fast—at least at the beginning. Leaders have to gather as many facts as they can as quickly
as possible (there are often few real facts at the start) and make initial decisions about the safety of their staff members and students.
Effective leaders teach themselves how to begin communicating,
even as they are taking control of the situation. Rarely is there the
luxury of getting everything in order before the reporters start to
call, parents arrive at school to retrieve their children, or the first
elected official inquires what is being done.

Most critical incidents last for more than one school day. Reporters
continue to call to see if counselors are still seeing kids, and parents
continue to seek reassurance that it is safe to send their children
back to school. Therefore, crises call for ongoing, information-laden,

and comforting communication—often long after things seem normal inside the school and you have turned your mind to other concerns. (It is easy to forget that those outside the school walls do not have the comfort of hearing the class bells and seeing the students move through the building—of seeing that things really are back to normal.)

The web and social media provide school leaders with quick, easy-to-use means of communication that are, perhaps most importantly, *sustainable over time*. Putting out even a one-page backpack newssheet every day for a week (as we used to do after a school fire or during an outbreak of meningitis) is a communication method that quickly collapses under its own weight. But posting a short website or Facebook update or sending a Tweet can keep parents and community feeling up-to-date with minimal effort.

Building and Maintaining Trust

Beyond securing the safety and well-being of students and staff members, the chief job of the leader in a critical incident is maintaining the community's trust. With any luck, you have been fostering relationships within your community for years. In a crisis, you can draw on that trust.

But suppose you are a principal or superintendent new to the building or community. The crisis offers you both the challenge and the opportunity to build trust at lightning speed. You have little choice but to step up to the plate. We've known principals and superintendents who've come through difficult situations in their new communities with flying colors and shiny reputations that might have taken them years to develop under normal circumstances. We have also known leaders to crash and burn under the pressure.

One of the main differences between success and disaster is the willingness and the ability to communicate early and often with stakeholders, not only during the first hours of the crisis but also in the longer days that follow. When stakeholders hear from their leader regularly during uncertain times, they tend to think that the leader is doing a good job.

As we well know, "trust is, of course, hard to come by and easy to lose" (Boin et al., 2008, p. 61). How you communicate what you know—and what you *don't* know—is key to maintaining the trust of your entire community, including your students, staff members, parents, neighbors, elected officials, business partners, and even the reporters at your door.

Act Fast, and Act Early

When a child has been injured or a bus is involved in an accident, it may take days (or even weeks) to sort out exactly what happened, but a leader can't afford to wait until he or she knows all the details. Early reports need to be labeled as early reports—but these days, they need to go out *early*. Stakeholders who have come to expect eyewitness news from events in Syria, Pakistan, or Japan expect no less from their school district. If you don't supply the information, someone else will fill the airwaves, perhaps with less accurate, and more damaging, information than you.

A Twitter feed like the one at the beginning of this chapter, text messages relayed to all parents, and frequent postings on the district web or Facebook page provide staff, parents, and community members with a level of comfort that allows you time to get the work done. The following are some examples of messages you might post:

- "All the students have been accounted for and returned to their classrooms. HAZMAT team has sealed off the lab wing and is investigating. No word on the cause."

- "Four third graders have been transported to the hospital with NON-life-threatening injuries. Parents have been notified. All other children may be picked up AT SCHOOL."

- "Fire department investigating cause of the fire. School will be closed tomorrow. Alternative learning sites are being identified. Stay tuned for details."

Messages such as these provide immediate, helpful information and comfort anxious parents even though they contain little concrete information about the event (perhaps because there is none yet). Messages like these—sent early and often—head off rumors, leaks, and ominous silences. They announce that you are in charge and are making wise decisions. They build trust.

A Dance of Opposites

In today's world, crisis management is a dance between *collaboration* (the expectation of our young parents and staff) and *command and control* (the swift actions needed to stop further damage and provide immediate safety for everyone involved). In most communities today, authority never goes unquestioned, yet anyone who has lived through a life-threatening emergency knows you cannot manage a critical incident by committee.

To respond to this tug of war, effective crisis communication demands creativity, improvisation, and flexibility. Although parents cannot dictate the conditions of an emergency parent-child reunification process, leaders can provide access to information about the difficulties involved, the resources being brought to bear, and the decisions being made—*as they are being made*. Social media and web technologies lend themselves to this kind of communication.

Another anomaly is that although you may be creating messages on the fly and changing the media you use to fit the situation, the school systems that are the most effective in communicating during a crisis are those that have already institutionalized their communication procedures. Staff, parents, and even connected community members already know where to look to find reliable and timely information about what is happening in their school. No time is lost searching for word from the school or district. There is already a well-known public face for school news.

Now is the time to set up your Twitter feed. *Now* is the time to create your Facebook community. Don't wait for chaos to strike before you begin to use YouTube. If people know they will find you at these locations and trust what you are telling them, they will listen.

Making Meaning in a Crisis

In *The Politics of Crisis Management,* Boin et al. (2008) define a crisis as the point at which a disturbance is so large that the system is unable to cope. At that point, the core values of the organization come under threat, and the community feels a high degree of uncertainty.

In these situations—these researchers report and our experience confirms—people immediately look to their leader to make decisions quickly and communicate those decisions clearly. Today, we would add, people are also looking for an immediate assignment of responsibility. The questions the public asks are:

- What happened?
- Why did it happen?
- What are you going to do?
- Who is to blame?
- How can we be sure it won't happen again?

The bystanders, and even the participants, in any critical incident can only see a small corner of the event. Their view is limited by their vantage point. The community is asking the leader to put the pieces together and make meaning of the whole, and they are no longer willing to wait for answers. They begin asking these questions immediately.

As a result, however, the leader has an opportunity to shape people's understanding of what happened and, coincidentally, to build support around his or her solutions from the beginning. It is a unique opportunity, and woe to the leader who does not accept the challenge. There is sure to be someone else in the community who is more than willing to offer another version of the story and assign blame.

School leaders cannot rely on their crisis management performance to speak for itself. The facts—such as the staff members responsible for the test irregularities have been identified and dealt with according to personnel regulations, the students who threatened violence have been removed from the school, or the entire student body was safely evacuated and no one was hurt—in and of themselves will not convince the naysayers.

It's up to the leader to communicate the whole story—including the satisfactory, and in some cases courageous, resolution to the issue. The leader must help the community understand why and how it happened as well as what remedial steps have been taken to solve the problem. This is how the leader makes meaning and manages the district's reputation.

Evaluating Results Over Time

The event is not over when the crisis itself has ended. Depending on the severity of the crisis, healing can take weeks or even months. During that time, only in the after-action reviews will you be able to gauge the effectiveness of your communication efforts. The aftermath of a crisis is a good time to take stock of all your strategic communication practices by asking:

- Which communication tools reached the widest audiences?
- Which communication tools were best able to reach targeted groups of stakeholders?
- Did your community understand your messages?
- Were the messages effective?
- How do you know?

What you learn from these reviews will help you shape communication for your school or district going forward. This is a time, as the organization rebuilds its stability, when great lessons can be learned and progress can be made. Web and Facebook pages, Twitter feeds, text messages—along with video clips, community comment, and media reporting—provide a permanent and visible record of leadership. Together they help to create meaning.

Next Steps

1. Dust off your school or district crisis plan. Examine the crisis communication section. How can social media enhance your effectiveness?

2. Gather the people who would be lead players in a critical incident, and work together to rewrite the pieces of the plan that need updating.

Key Points

Social media is tailor-made for communicating during a critical incident; it's fast, flexible, easy to use, and sustainable over time. Social media gives the school leader a chance to frame the message around a crisis before outsiders attempt to take control. Social media offers leaders the ability to create meaning around the event for stakeholders—an important step in reestablishing a normal life in the community.

12 The New World: It's Just the Beginning

Writing about social media is like changing the proverbial tire on a moving bus. Even before this manuscript gets to print, there will be more gadgets, more apps, and new ways to stay in touch. There will also be more choices. The next generation of communication devices will be even more mobile—smaller, faster, and more adept—than the ones we use now. We will carry all our connections with us as we go.

Having gotten ourselves this far, no doubt we will soon have to adapt to another new set of tools to get our messages to younger parents and teachers, without totally losing the over-forty crowd. Tomorrow—when YouTube is considered slow and cumbersome and Facebook has gone the way of the push lawn mower—we will have to employ technologies not yet invented to build relationships with our stakeholders.

The essential skills for the 21st century turn out to be flexibility and the ability to perform triage. As we move forward, we must continuously ask, Which of all these communication choices is the one (or ones) that will best serve our stakeholders? Which will get the job done? Being able and willing to make these choices is vital to good leadership.

Although the answers to these questions are not immutable, there are signposts.

It's Not About the Toys

We've said this before, but it bears repeating. Some of us do not care about the latest high-speed gizmo or the newest app, but many of us are charmed by the glitz. Aside from any education or communication value, it's just plain fun to have the newest, shiniest red wagon on the block. We suffer from SOS (Shiny Object Syndrome). There is no harm in that.

But when it comes to building a robust communication infrastructure for your stakeholders, the trick is keeping your eyes on the prize.

- Who are you trying to reach with your messages?
- How do these folks communicate? How do they reach each other?
- What messages are you trying to send?
- How quickly do you need to reach your stakeholders?
- What are you trying to persuade them to do?

Answering these questions today will help you decide whether to invest in a robust outbound bilingual telephone calling system or teach your staff how to use Twitter to reach their parents. Tomorrow, the choices and the answers may be different. One day at a time.

There Are No Right Answers

There are only better ones for your community. Making good decisions about how you use any new media in your school or district requires that you ask questions of all your stakeholders and really listen to what they have to tell you. Good communication these days starts with collaboration. It requires you to design a communication framework based on the best information you can collect and institutionalize that framework by using it constantly. It also requires that you be flexible and ready to change the framework when it stops working.

If ninety percent of your parents get their news from web and email, that's where you should put your resources. If mobile phones are your parents' connections to their world, forget the printed letters (or even the blogs) and learn to put your messages in 140-character chunks—even if those chunks are written in Spanish.

Social Media Is an Attitude

The ideas, explicit or implied, in these pages—collaboration, listening, flexibility, brevity, speed, client focus, and clarity—together describe a vision of communication between school and community that empowers school leaders to meet the demands of today's parents, staff members, neighbors, and community leaders.

The new technologies offer effective tools to get the job done. For best results, however, you must pair the tools with a new attitude. The community's demand for transparency is real. The tools will help you get there, but you must be willing to engage in the conversation. The tools alone—although they may provide you with a flashy cover for a while—will not stand the test of time.

Our recommendation is that you step out and take the risk. Team up with your staff members, parents, and community partners in the new ways that the technologies make possible. Use the power that collaboration generates to support teaching and learning for your students. We believe you will not be disappointed.

Next Steps

1. Make contact with three superintendents or principals who are using social media effectively. Send each an email. Ask how they got started. Ask one of them to be your mentor.

2. Convene a small communication advisory team in your school or district and call a meeting.

Key Points

How you use social media in your school or district depends on your community, on your comfort level with technology, and your ability to lead change. Just like implementing a new curriculum, it requires sweat equity on the front end. But as with a new curriculum, stronger relationships among the adults in a school community yield better learning results for its students. It's a collaborative effort, and there are no guarantees—but there are already enough of your colleagues out there that you won't be alone.

What Do You Think?

The conversation about school communications in the digital age continues. Please join us at our website, www.porterfieldandcarnes.com, and tell us what you think.

References and Resources

American Association of School Administrators. (2009). [Social media survey]. Unpublished raw data.

American Association of School Administrators. (2011). [Focus group]. Unpublished raw data.

Anderson, J., & Rainie, L. (2010). *Future of the Internet IV* [Abstract]. Accessed at www.pewinternet.org/Reports/2010/Future-of-the -Internet-IV.aspx on May 25, 2011.

Boin, A., 't Hart, P., Stern, E., & Sundelius, B. (2008). *The politics of crisis management: Public leadership under pressure.* Cambridge, England: Cambridge University Press.

Booth, S. (2008). Technology use in independent schools: Highlights from the 2007 NAIS technology survey. *Independent School Magazine, 67*(2). Accessed at www.nais.org/publications/ismagazinearticle .cfm?ItemNumber=151426 on May 4, 2011.

Boudreaux, C. (2011). *Social media governance: Policy database.* Accessed at http://socialmediagovernance.com/policies.php on May 29, 2011.

Brisbane, A. S. (2011, May 7). The White House's bedtime bombshell. *New York Times.* Accessed at www.nytimes.com/2011/05/08 /opinion/08pubed.html?_r=1 on November 18, 2011.

Britten, D. (2011a, March 11). The end of common sense in Lansing? [Web log post]. Accessed at http://colonelb.posterous.com/the-end- of-common-sense-in-lansing on September 1, 2011.

Britten, D. (2011b, March 20). A rising or setting sun on K–12 education? [Web log post]. Accessed at http://colonelb.posterous.com/a-rising -or-setting-sun-on-k-12-education on September 1, 2011.

Brogan, C., & Smith, J. (2010). *Trust agents: Using the web to build influence, improve reputation, and earn trust.* San Francisco: Wiley.

Bushaw, W. J., & Lopez., S. J. (2010). A time for change: The 42nd annual Phil Delta Kappa/Gallup poll of the public's attitudes toward the public schools. *Phi Delta Kappan, 92*(1), 9–26. Accessed at www.pdkintl.org/kappan/docs/2010_Poll_Report.pdf on May 21, 2011.

Carozza, B. (2011, March 4). Converted to online learning [Web log post]. Accessed at http://billcarozza.com/2011/03/04/online -learning/ on September 1, 2011.

Chesterfield County Public Schools. (n.d.). In *Facebook* [Education page]. Accessed at www.facebook.com/chesterfieldschools on May 21, 2011.

Chilcott, L. (Executive Producer), & Guggenheim, D. (Co-Writer/ Director). (2010). *Waiting for "Superman"* [Motion picture]. United States: Walden Media.

Cision. (2010). National survey finds majority of journalists now depend on social media for story research [Press release]. Accessed at http: //us.cision.com/news_room/press_releases/2010/2010-1-20_gwu _survey.asp on November 18, 2011.

comScore. (2011). *The 2010 digital year in review.* Accessed at www .comscore.com/Press_Events/Presentations_Whitepapers/2011 /2010_US_Digital_Year_in_Review on May 21, 2011.

Dugan, L. (2011). *Twitter beats gov't, traditional media and geologi- cal organizations to break #earthquake news.* Accessed at www. mediabistro.com/alltwitter/twitter-beats-govt-traditional-media -and-geological-organizations-to-break-earthquake-news_b13016 on September 14, 2011.

Facebook. (2011). *Create a page.* Accessed at www.facebook.com/pages /create.php on May 22, 2011.

Fox, S. (2011). *Americans living with disability and their technology profile* [Abstract.] Accessed at http://pewinternet.org/Search. aspx?q=americans%20living%20with%20disability%20and%20 their%20technology%20profile on May 4, 2011.

Fullan, M. (2001). *Leading in a culture of change.* San Francisco: Jossey-Bass.

Gladwell, M. (2000). *The tipping point: How little things can make a big difference.* Boston: Little, Brown.

Godfrey-Lee Public Schools. (n.d.). In *Facebook* [Public school page]. Accessed at www.facebook.com/LeeRebels on March 15, 2011.

Godin, S. (2008). *Tribes: We need you to lead us.* New York: Portfolio Hardcover.

Godin, S. (2011). *Seth Godin's blog.* Accessed at http://sethgodin .typepad.com on September 14, 2011.

Goleman, D. (1998). *Working with emotional intelligence* [Google reader]. New York: Bantam Books. Accessed at www.google.com on May 21, 2011.

Heath, C., & Heath, D. (2007). *Made to stick: Why some ideas survive and others die.* New York: Random House.

Heath, C., & Heath, D. (2010). *Switch: How to change things when change is hard.* New York: Crown Business.

Howe, N., Strauss, W., & Nadler, R. (2008). *Millennials & K–12 schools: Educational strategies for a new generation.* Great Falls, VA: LifeCourse.

Hunt, T. (2009). *The whuffie factor: Using the power of social networks to build your business.* New York: Crown Business.

Idle, N., & Nunns, A. (Eds.). (2011). *Tweets from Tahrir: Egypt's revolution as it unfolded, in the words of the people who made it.* New York: OR Books.

Jayson, S. (2010, December 30). 2010: The year we stopped talking. *USA Today,* pp. 1–2.

Kang, C., & Thompson, K. (2011, February 23). Hispanics on web less than others. *The Washington Post,* p. A11.

Kotter, J. P. (2008). *Leading change.* Boston: Harvard Business Press.

Knight Foundation. (2010). *Knight soul of the community 2010: Why people love where they live and why it matters: A national perspective.* Accessed at www.soulofthecommunity.org/sites/default/files /OVERALL.pdf on May 31, 2011.

Kraft, J. (2011a, January 14). Hello, young man! [Web log post]. Accessed at http://providenceschool.wordpress.com/?s=Hello%2C +Young+Man on September 1, 2011.

Kraft, J. (2011b, January 28). We miss you! [Web log post]. Accessed at http://providenceschool.wordpress.com/2011/01/28/we-miss-you on September 1, 2011.

Kraft, J. (2011c, March 18). Love letter to our PTA [Web log post]. Accessed at http://providenceschool.wordpress.com/2011/03/18 /love-letter-to-our-pta/ on September 1, 2011.

Kurtz, J. (2009 November). *Getting started: Listening and developing your social media policy* presented at the Chesapeake Chapter of the National School Public Relations Association Fall Conference, Frederick, MD.

Lamott, A. (1995). *Bird by bird: Some instructions on writing and life.* New York: Anchor Books.

Leadership success interview. (1999). Princeton, NJ: Gallup Leadership Institute.

Lehmann, C. (2010a, February 25). Technology and the whole child [Web log post]. Accessed at http://practicaltheory.org/serendipity /index.php?/archives/1294-Technology-and-the-Whole-Child.html on September 1, 2011.

Lehmann, C. (2010b, March 7). An important win [Web log post]. Accessed at http://practicaltheory.org/serendipity/index.php? /archives/1295-An-Important-Win.html on September 1, 2011.

Lehmann, C. (2010c, March 9). Save the National Writing Project [Web log post]. Accessed at http://practicaltheory.org/serendipity /index.php?/archives/1230-Save-the-National-Writing-Project.html on September 1, 2011.

Lehrer, J. (2009). *How we decide.* Boston: Houghton Mifflin Harcourt.

Lenhart, A. (2010). *Cell phones and American adults* [Abstract]. Accessed at www.pewinternet.org/Reports/2010/Cell-Phones-and -American-Adults.aspx on May 21, 2011.

Li, C., & Bernoff, J. (2008). *Groundswell: Winning in a world transformed by social technologies*. Boston: Harvard Business Press.

Louis, K. S., Leithwood, K., Wahlstrom, K. L., & Anderson, S. E. (2010). *Investigating the links to improved student learning: Final report of research findings*. St. Paul: University of Minnesota. Accessed at www.cehd.umn.edu/carei/Leadership/Learning-from -Leadership_Final-Research-Report_July-2010.pdf on April 25, 2011.

Madden, M. (2010). *Older adults and social media* [Abstract]. Accessed at http://pewresearch.org/pubs/1711/older-adults-social-networking -facebook-twitter on September 14, 2011.

Marklein, M. B. (2011, May 4). Survey: Educators lack training to teach online. *USA Today*. Accessed at www.usatoday.com/tech /news/2011–05–04-online-safety-students-schools_n.htm on September 14, 2011.

Moran, P. (2011a, February 21). 18 Presidents: On education [Web log post]. Accessed at http://spacesforlearning.wordpress.com/2011 /02/21/18-presidents-on-education/ on September 1, 2011.

Moran, P. (2011b, March 17). I write for Savannah [Web log post]. Accessed at http://spacesforlearning.wordpress.com/2011/03/17 /i-write-for-savannah-blog4nwp/ on September 1, 2011.

Mui, Y. Q., & Whoriskey, P. (2010, December 31). Facebook cements no. 1 status. *The Washington Post*, p. A12.

National School Public Relations Association. (2011). *Communications survey: Results and analysis* [PowerPoint presentation]. Accessed at www.nspra.org/2011capsurvey on September 14, 2011.

New Milford High School. (2011). In *Facebook* [Public school page]. Accessed at www.facebook.com/pages/New-Milford-High-School /103758836330278 on March 15, 2011.

November, A. C. (2010). *Empowering students with technology*. Thousand Oaks, CA: Corwin Press.

O'Reilly, T., & Milstein, S. (2009). *The Twitter book*. Sebastopol, CA: O'Reilly Media.

Olmert, M. D. (2009). *Made for each other: The biology of the human-animal bond*. Cambridge, MA: Da Capo Press.

Park Hill School District. (n.d.). In *Guidelines* [Public school page]. Accessed at www.facebook.com/ParkHillSchoolDistrict?sk=app_4949752878? on March 15, 2011.

Patch. (2011). *About us*. Accessed at www.patch.com/about on May 21, 2011.

Pegoraro, R. (2011a, January 2). Smartphones ruled the year, connecting users as never before. *The Washington Post*. Accessed at http://www.washingtonpost.com/wp-dyn/content/article/2011/01/01/AR2011010102091.html on January 3, 2012.

Pegoraro, R. (2011b, January 8). Crowds signal a CES resurgence. *The Washington Post*, p. A6.

Pew Research Center. (2008). *Internet overtakes newspapers as news outlet: Biggest stories of 2008—Economy tops campaign*. Accessed at http://people-press.org/2008/12/23/internet-overtakes-newspapers-as-news-outlet on May 4, 2011.

Pew Research Center. (2010). *Americans spending more time following the news: Ideological news sources—Who watches and why* [Abstract]. Accessed at http://pewresearch.org/pubs/1725/where-people-get-news-print-online-readership-cable-news-viewers on May 4, 2011.

Phi Delta Kappa. (2009). *PDK/Gallup poll on the public's attitudes toward public schools*. Accessed at www.pdkintl.org/kappan/pastpolls on May 31, 2011.

Pinnington, D. (2011). Essential dos and don'ts for Twitter users. *LawPRO Magazine, 10*(1). Accessed at http://www.practicepro.ca/LAWPROMag/TwitterDosDonts.pdf on May 21, 2011.

Pollitt, C. (2011). *How the US Air Force constructs social media policy*. Accessed at http://socialmediatoday.com/johnmctigue/293715/how-us-air-force-constructs-social-media-policy on May 21, 2011.

Porterfield, K., & Carnes, M. (2008). *Why school communication matters: Strategies from PR professionals.* Lanham, MD: Rowman & Littlefield Education.

Porterfield, K., & Carnes, M. (2011). Twitter: Not just about ham sandwiches. *Educational Leadership, 68*(8). Accessed at www.ascd .org/publications/educational-leadership/may11/vol68/num08 /Twitter@-Not-Just-About-Ham-Sandwiches.aspx on February 21, 2012.

Purcell, K., Rainie, L., Mitchell, A., Rosenstiel, T., & Olmstead, K. (2010). *Understanding the participatory news consumer* [Abstract]. Accessed at http://pewinternet.org/Reports/2010/Online-News .aspx on September 14, 2011.

Rubel, S. (2011). *Editorial reviews.* Accessed at www.amazon.com /Twitter-Book-Tim-OReilly/dp/0596802811 on May 29, 2011.

Salem-Keizer Public Schools. (2011). In *Facebook* [Public school page]. Accessed at www.facebook.com/salemkeizerschools on March 15, 2011.

Schwarz, R. (2011, May 27). Friday faux pas: Teacher loses tenure over Facebook postings [Web log post]. Accessed at http://socialmedia .mayoclinic.org/2011/05/27/friday-faux-pas-teacher-loses-tenure -over-facebook-postings on September 14, 2011.

Smith, A. (2010a). *Broadband 2010: A big slowdown.* Accessed at http://pewresearch.org/pubs/1694/broadband-adoption-slows -dramatically-except-african-americans-little-interest-among-non-users on May 21, 2011.

Smith, A. (2010b). *Americans and their gadgets: Cell phones.* Accessed at www.pewinternet.org/Reports/2010/Gadgets/Report/Cell-phones .aspx on May 4, 2011.

Smith, A. (2010c). *Technology trends among people of color.* Accessed at http://pewinternet.org/commentary/2010/september/technology -trends-among-people-of-color on May 4, 2011.

Smith, M. (2011). Mari Smith [Web log post]. Accessed at www .marismith.com/mari-smith-blog on September 14, 2011.

Stewart, J. (2011, March 3). I am thankful to be a teacher [Web log post]. Accessed at http://drjstewart.wordpress.com/2011/03/03/i -am-thankful-to-be-a-teacher/ on September 1, 2011.

Strauss, W., & Howe, N. (1991). *Generations: The history of America's future, 1584 to 2069.* New York: Morrow.

Taylor, P., & Wang, W. (2010). *The fading glory of the television and telephone* [Abstract]. Accessed at http://pewresearch.org/pubs/1702 /luxury-necessity-television-landline-cell-phone on May 4, 2011.

Townsend, C. (2011). *Misinformation on hyperlocal news sites like AOL's Patch.com and NJ.com causes challenges for the Summit board of education.* Accessed at http://thealternativepress.com/articles /misinformation-on-hyperlocal-news-sites-like-aol%E2%80%99s -patchcom-and-njcom-causes-challenges-for-the-summit-board-of -education on November 18, 2011.

Union County Public Schools. (n.d.). In *Welcome* [Public school page]. Accessed at www.facebook.com/ucps.nc on March 15, 2011.

Vanderbilt University. (2011). *What is social media?* Accessed at http:// web.vanderbilt.edu/i/VUSocialMediaHandbook.pdf on May 21, 2011.

Wasik, B. (2010). *And then there's this: How stories live and die in a viral culture.* New York: Penguin.

West, D. M., Whitehurst, G. J., & Dionne, E. J., Jr. (2011). *Americans want more coverage of teacher performance and student achievement.* Accessed at www.brookings.edu/reports/2011/0329_education _news.aspx on May 21, 2011.

Whitby, T. (2011, April 2). World's simplest online safety policy [Web log post]. Accessed at http://tomwhitby.wordpress.com/2011/04/02 /world%E2%80%99s-simplest-online-safety-policy/ on May 21, 2011.

Wright, S., & Page, E. C. (2009). *2009 women and social media study.* Accessed at www.blogher.com/files/2009_Compass_BlogHer _Social_Media_Study_042709_FINAL.pdf on May 21, 2011.

Wood, G. (2011). *George Wood's blog.* Accessed at www.forumforeducation .org/blogs/george-wood on September 15, 2011.

Zeithaml, V. A., & Bitner, M. J. (1996). *Services marketing.* New York: McGraw-Hill.

Zickuhr, K. (2010). *Generations online in 2010.* Accessed at http://pewresearch.org/pubs/1831/generations-online-2010 on May 4, 2011.

Zickuhr, K. (2011). *Generations and their gadgets* [Abstract]. Accessed at http://pewinternet.org/reports/2011/generations-and-gadgets.aspx on May 4, 2011.

Index

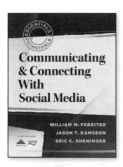

Communicating & Connecting With Social Media
William M. Ferriter, Jason T. Ramsden, and Eric C. Sheninger

In this short text, the authors examine how enterprising schools are using social media tools to provide customized professional development for teachers and to transform communication practices with staff, students, parents, and other stakeholders.
BKF474

Personal Learning Networks
Using the Power of Connections to Transform Education
Will Richardson and Rob Mancabelli

Follow this road map for using the web for learning. Learn how to build your own learning network. Use learning networks in the classroom and make the case for schoolwide learning networks to improve student outcomes.
BKF484

The Connected Educator
Learning and Leading in a Digital Age
Sheryl Nussbaum-Beach and Lani Ritter Hall

Create a connected learning community through social media and rediscover the power of being a learner first. The authors show you how to take advantage of technology to collaborate with other educators and deepen the learning of your students.
BKF478

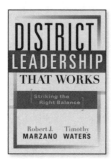

District Leadership That Works
Striking the Right Balance
Robert J. Marzano and Timothy Waters

Bridge the divide between administrative duties and daily classroom impact with a leadership mechanism called "defined autonomy." Learn strategies for creating district-defined goals while giving building-level staff the stylistic freedom to respond quickly and effectively to student failure.
BKF314

a division of

Solution Tree | Press
Solution Tree

Visit solution-tree.com or call 800.733.6786 to order.

Solution Tree | Press

a division of

Solution Tree

Solution Tree's mission is to advance the work of our authors. By working with the best researchers and educators worldwide, we strive to be the premier provider of innovative publishing, in-demand events, and inspired professional development designed to transform education to ensure that all students learn.

THE SCHOOL SUPERINTENDENTS ASSOCIATION

The American Association of School Administrators, founded in 1865, is the professional organization for more than 13,000 educational leaders across the United States. AASA advocates for the highest quality public education for all students, and develops and supports school system leaders.